Charles A. Beard

An Observance of the Centennial of His Birth

DePauw University
Greencastle, Indiana
October 11-12, 1974

Edited by Marvin C. Swanson

The Charles A. Beard Centennial
was sponsored by
DePauw University

Copies of these Proceedings may be
purchased from
DePauw University, Greencastle,
Indiana 46135 for $1.50 per copy.

Contents

Preface

Later in his life, Charles Beard once wrote to James T. Farrell, "I wish you would mention the fact that the faculty of Old DePauw did more for me than I could ever tell." While a student is attending college, it is so often difficult to know how much influence the faculty and total institution are having on him. As one prominent alumnus of DePauw, Beard certainly felt that his alma mater was most influential and contributed much to his life. In time, Beard went on to make his own contribution to the American story, becoming an outstanding interpreter of American history and political ideas.

His wife, Mary Ritter Beard, also a DePauw graduate contributed greatly to Beard's prolific pen. These two intellectual giants occasioned the symposium to mark the centennial of Beard's birth. The natural outcome of this event in October, 1974, is this volume, comprising the three scholarly lectures and other materials which contribute so much to our renewed appreciation of Charles and Mary Beard.

It is not possible to list all of the individuals who have participated in the coordination of this significant occasion on the DePauw campus. However, on behalf of the University, I would take this opportunity to express our sincere gratitude to the Centennial Committee, the History Department, the visiting lecturers, and especially to the members of the Beard family for their participation in the Centennial events and their assistance in providing primary source materials.

With the Bicentennial of our nation at hand, we at DePauw University hope that this volume on Charles A. Beard will contribute to a clearer understanding and appreciation of Beard's life and thoughts as well as of Americans as a leading nation and people of the world.

William E. Kerstetter
Chancellor of the University

April, 1976

Charles A. Beard
1874-1948

Charles A. Beard, 1874-1948

Charles A. Beard, one of the most influential historians of the twentieth century, was born one hundred years ago on a farm in Henry County, Indiana, on November 27, 1874. After attending a small Quaker academy in nearby Spiceland, he spent almost four years as joint publisher and editor with his older brother of a small-town weekly, the Knightstown *Sun*. In the spring of 1895 he matriculated at DePauw University in Greencastle, where he majored in history, political science, and sociology, and enjoyed an active campus career as an intercollegiate orator, debater, and editor of the student newspaper. Here he also met his future wife, Mary Ritter, who became his lifelong collaborator and the co-author with him of several important historical works.

Graduating from DePauw in 1898, Beard went to England to continue his study of history at Oxford, where he helped to found a workingmen's institute, Ruskin Hall. He traveled widely throughout England's Mid-lands, lecturing to labor groups and recruiting students for Ruskin Hall, and with his wife toured the European continent before returning to the United States. Upon completing his Ph.D. at Columbia University in 1902, Beard stayed on as a popular teacher of history and political science until his abrupt resignation in October, 1917, over the issue of freedom of speech in wartime.

Charles A. Beard spent the rest of his life largely outside academic walls in such activities as working for municipal reform in New York City, advising political leaders in Japan, investigating conditions in Yugoslavia, testifying before congressional committees, and carrying on an immense amount of scholarly research and writing. In addition to a large number of miscellaneous writings, he was the author or co-author of forty-nine books in history and related fields, ranging from *An Economic Interpretation of the Constitution* (1913) to the classic *Rise of American Civilization* (2 vols., 1927; with Mary R. Beard) and his last and most controversial volume, *President Roosevelt and the Coming of the War, 1941* (1948). As an indication of the breadth of his scholarly interests and the high regard of his fellow scholars, he was elected to preside over both the American Political Science Association and the American Historical Association.

Symposium Marks
the Birth of Charles A. Beard

Fredrick L. Bergmann

Old DePauw and New—alumni, faculty, trustees and administration, and old friends; younger members of the faculty and the student body—joined in October to celebrate with the Beard family and a group of noted historians the centennial of the birth of Charles A. Beard, DePauw alumnus, 1898. It was the third major symposium to be held on Old Gold Day in the past six years.

Center of attention in the centennial celebration was the man who, according to Henry Steele Commager, distinguished American historian and one of the three major speakers on the program, "had more influence, not only on history and the teaching of history but possibly on the whole course of public affairs, than any other academic in the first half of the twentieth century."

Dr. William E. Kerstetter, President of the University, opened the convocation with an appreciation of the celebrated historian and of his wife, Mary Ritter, also a DePauw graduate and a noted historian who was Beard's co-author in many of his works. The fame and the continuing significance of the ideas of Charles and Mary Beard occasioned, President Kerstetter indicated, the scholarly symposium on the centennial anniversary of Charles Beard's birth.

Chancellor William E. Kerstetter talks with DePauw Professor of History James L. Cooper and Dr. Eugene D. Genovese, Chairman of the History Department at the University of Rochester and one of the speakers during the Charles A. Beard Symposium.

Joining with DePauw in celebration of the centennial anniversary of Charles A. Beard's birth were symposium speakers (left to right) Dr. John Braeman, Dr. Eugene D. Genovese, and Dr. Henry Steele Commager; William Beard and Mrs. Miriam Vagts, son and daughter of Charles Beard; Professor Detlev Vagts, a grandson; and Gordon Ritter, a nephew.

Eminent historians who joined Dr. Commager, who was Beard's successor as Professor of History at Columbia University and who is now on the faculty of Amherst College, were Dr. Eugene Genovese, Professor of History and chairman of the history department at the University of Rochester, and Dr. John Braeman, Professor of History at the University of Nebraska. The three are recognized as giants in the field of American history.

The Beard Family

Center of attention during the week-end celebration were the descendents of Charles and Mary Beard. These included Dr. William Beard, their son, whose distinguished career includes teaching posts at Cal Tech and the University of Wisconsin and the authorship of more than a dozen books; Mrs. Miriam Vagts, their daughter, who has done research and writing on the life and works of her illustrious parents; and Beard's grandson, Professor Detlev Vagts of the Harvard University School of Law, who spoke for the family at the centennial banquet.

Other members of the family who attended the symposium were Gordon T. Ritter of Columbus, Ind., Mrs. Beard's nephew; G.M. "Binx" Walker of Jackson, Miss., son of Mrs. Beard's niece; Mrs. Henry Beard of Zionsville, Ind., whose husband was Beard's nephew; her two sons, Charles Beard of Indianapolis and Henry Beard of Carmel, Ind.; and Henry's son Richard.

Charles Beard, Historian and Critic

Charles Beard was born on November 27, 1874, on a farm near Knightstown, Ind., to which his father had moved from the South when the Civil War broke out. As a high-school graduate at the age of 17, he started, with his brother Clarence, a weekly newspaper, The Knightstown *Sun*. Four years later, having decided to become a

Miriam Vagts and William Beard, daughter and son of Charles A. Beard, and Detlev Vagts, his grandson, (right), were among those attending the two-day session at the Gobin United Methodist Church honoring the late historian.

minister, he enrolled in DePauw University, where he excelled in campus oratory and journalism and shifted his interests to history and political science. He was graduated in three years, having accelerated his course with two summer sessions, including one at Chicago's Hull House, a period of study which made a lasting impression on him.

Another lasting impression was his involvement with campus journalism. As editor of the school newspaper, the *DePauw Palladium* , in his senior year, he confirmed his dedication to searching for truth. His last editorial, published in May, 1898, and quoted by Professor John Baughman of the Department of History during the symposium, reads as follows:

> There is but one way to know the truth, and that is not a golden one. It is fraught with toil and sacrifice and perhaps ridicule. The seeker of the truth must be

fearless and must not be afraid to enter the innermost holies of holies, and to tear down the veils of superstition that hang about any human and so-called divine institution. It is the truth that makes men free...And this truth only will be known when...men begin to seek the truth in the records of history, politics, and religion and science.

This young man was recognized in the yearbook, *The Mirage,* that year as one of the "Big Five" on the campus and referred to as a "Prohibopopulistic orator." Quite obviously his future was determined before he left DePauw.

Beard went to England upon graduation, studied at Oxford, helped to found Ruskin Hall, a workingmen's college at Oxford, married Mary Ritter, '97, who had taught school in Greencastle following her graduation, earned the Ph.D. degree from Columbia University in 1904, and immediately became a lecturer in history there. He stayed on the faculty thirteen years, resigning in 1917 on an issue of academic freedom when three colleagues were ousted because of their anti-war sentiments.

His fame both at home and abroad began in 1913 with the publication of *An Economic Interpretation of the Constitution of the United States,* an intellectual bombshell in which Beard questioned the motives of the Founding Fathers, claiming that the Constitution protected the commercial interests and property rights of the framers and their friends. The book brought Beard both praise and a storm of criticism and launched him on a career which included the publication of notable works of history, promotion of education for workers in New York City, the founding of the New School for Social Research, advising the Japanese government on the reconstruction of Tokyo after the disastrous earthquake of 1924, and lecturing throughout the world.

The steady stream of books included several joint productions of Charles and Mary, including *The Rise of American Civilization* (1927), in which the reader discerns

Mary's fervent feminism, and their most popular book *A Basic History of the United States* (1944), which has been widely used as a textbook. The *Basic History* was another landmark in Beard's development as one of the nation's leading historians, for in it he and Mary Beard ignored the economic interpretation of the U.S. Constitution which had played a prominent role in his writings since the appearance of his *Economic Interpretation of the Constitution*. A great part of the centennial symposium centered upon consideration by the noted historians in attendance of Beard's shifting point of view during the course of his long career as historian and political critic.

The Centennial Program

The centennial celebration on the campus fell into two parts, one an appreciation of Charles Beard by President Kerstetter and by a spokesman for the Beard family, and the other a critical inquiry into the impact of Beard upon American historical writing by the distinguished historians invited to the symposium and by DePauw professors of history who joined in the scholarly discussions.

President Kerstetter, in opening the two-day celebration on the afternoon of October 11, stated the theme as a focus "on the life of this very distinguished and stimulating historian, who (we proudly remind you) with his wife, Mary Ritter, went to DePauw University and then on to their distinguished careers." At a centennial banquet that evening he introduced Mr. Detlev Vagts, a distinguished professor of law at Harvard University and grandson of Charles and Mary Beard, as spokesman for the Beard family. Professor Vagts is the son of Mrs. Alfred Vagts, daughter of the Beards.

Professor Vagts characterized his grandfather as typically Victorian in his confidence, his serenity, his assurance. "Even for a man who, like my grandfather, spent most of his life questioning, posing problems to people and to the discipline of history," Professor Vagts said, "there was an ultimate assurance that the game was worth playing, that the job was worth doing, and that a man could devote his life to pursuing. And this is something that one doesn't encounter too often nowadays." Charles Beard, he said, was "an outgoing man, but a man with a great deal of simplicity, despite the complexity of the life which he led those many years over many countries and continents."

"One of the strong, moving features of Grandfather's life was his love of this country," his grandson said. "He thought of the United States as a great and noble experiment, something unique and to some degree exempt from the things that had gone wrong elsewhere."

Symposium

Professor Genovese opened the symposium proper with an address in Gobin Memorial Church on "Beard's Economic Interpretation of History." In it he disavowed the theory—as Beard himself had done—that Beard was a Marxist and faulted him for "his inability to come to terms with the psychological dimension of history." Yet his books made undeniable contributions to our understanding of American history, Professor Genovese said. "He asked the big questions and set the terms for much of the debate," he said, reflecting on "the depth and breadth of his impact—on the extent to which he asked so many of the big questions with which we still grapple and on the extent to which he liberated American history from so much cant and trivia."

Later in the day Professor Braeman, speaking on "Charles A. Beard: Historian and Progressive," cited Beard's guiding principle as "to look at things coldly and realistically, rather than through the rosy spectacles of some dogmas satisfactory to inherited preconceptions."

"There was a streak of the gadfly, the irreverent, the iconoclast in Beard," he said, "a delight in deflating pretensions, in startling his audience, in puncturing the conventional wisdom." He quoted historian Carl Becker as characterizing Beard as both a "hard-headed idealist" and at the same time "an exasperated cynic and a warm-hearted friend of suffering humanity...too sophisticated not to delight in dispelling illusions, yet too humanely sympathetic to fall back into the easy cynicism of one who is content merely to observe the tragic comedy of existence."

"Throughout this life," Professor Braeman added, "Beard's overriding commitment was to the fulfillment of the promise of American life. The indispensable prerequisite was material abundance for all—'a high standard of life for the whole mass of the American people,'" in Beard's own words. The America of his dreams was a land "without the degradation of poverty and unemployment on the one side or the degradation of luxury, rivalry, and conspicuous waste on the other...a beautiful country—homes beautiful; communities and farms beautiful; stores and workshops beautiful." And he added ruefully, "Sheer utopianism, my masters will say. But without vision, men and women perish, nations perish."

Professor Braeman described the continuing tension in Beard between the scholar and the activist and his resolution of that tension by promoting reform through scholarship and writing. He was a life-long champion of civil liberties because of his commitment to preserving the free marketplace of ideas, the speaker said. Thus Beard wrote, "We could not expect to have liberty without some abuse of it," and "as between having too much authority or too much liberty, I preferred the latter." Yet he insisted that education inculcate in youth the basic values, that it should "instill in students knowledge of and respect for this country's distinctive and unique heritage."

Beard, Professor Braeman insisted, had "a deep respect and admiration for the wisdom and realism of the framers of the Constitution; yet his book *An Economic Interpretation of the Constitution*, in which he insisted that the Constitution was the work of the propertied few and designed to safeguard the economic interests of their class against popular majorities, was both denounced by the conservatives and hailed by reformers as "removing a major intellectual obstacle to their program of federal government action to regulate business and assist the less favored numbers of American society."

"What was Beard's legacy?" the speaker asked. "Even his sharpest critics admit that Beard was the most influential—indeed, the most seminal—figure in twentieth-century American historical thought."

Professor Commager, closing the series on Saturday with an address entitled "Charles A. Beard: A Study in Paradox," characterized Beard as "part of—and eventually spokesman for—that new pragmatic philosophy which swept over the country at the turn of the century, and which revolutionized not only science but philosophy, law, history, politics, even the arts." Beard was, he said, "the first major American historian to bring pragmatism—or functionalism—to bear on the interpretation of the past."

It is a mistake, Professor Commager insisted, to emphasize the iconoclastic quality of Beard's mind and character. "He was indeed a sceptic," he said, "and with something of the iconoclast in him. But he was even more a philosopher who wanted results, a reformer interested in change and progress. Romantic in his faith in progress, he was pragmatic in his methods of achieving it."

And as to Beard's seeming inconsistencies—his early internationalism, for example, compared with his later isolationism—Commager asked how a scholar who wrote indefatigably on so many subjects* could be held to a standard of consistency. The isolationism of his final years,

---

*One estimate of Beard's output is eight volumes of European history, twenty-one volumes of American history, fifteen textbooks (a total of 21,000 pages), and in addition another twenty thousand or so pages of articles and reviews.
(Professor Commager's note)

the speaker said, resulted from Beard's developed conviction that European totalitarianism was none of our concern, that the Old World was beyond redemption. "No American of his generation was more alert to threats against freedom, more responsive to the call for the defense of freedom, than Beard," he said, "but only on the domestic scene. He did not think that European freedom was worth fighting for."

In a panel discussion which followed, in which Dr. Clifton J. Phillips and Dr. John Baughman, professors of history, and senior history and English major Charles Ripley Tilden joined the three speakers, Professor Phillips characterized Beard as "a kind of consensus historian who saw the conflicts [in American history] as nonantagonistic contradictions within the particular American system, with its great genius for overcoming these kinds of contradictions in our constitutional system." Beard's economic interpretation of history, he said, "was not meant to be a general theory of economic or historical development because he was not a comparativist. Despite his early interest in English and European history, he saw America as the basic unit for study—at least for his historical studies—and did not make the kind of comparative analysis needed to produce a truly general theory of historical development."

Commenting on the seeming paradoxes in Beard's thinking, Professor Braeman insisted that they are not so paradoxical as they seem. "His ideas changed over time, in response to his reading, to his experience," he said.

Summing up, Professor Genovese said that it is impossible for any historian not to absorb all kinds of things from Beard's work. "As a mark of a really great and influential historian, after all his pet theories have been discarded and new facts have been brought up, the question is how much of his life's work has passed into the mainstream of historical interpretation," he said. Just as historians of ancient Rome are, in spite of new developments, ever infected by the work of Edward

Gibbon, so American historians are in all sorts of subtle ways influenced by Beard's contributions. Added Professor Commager, "Beard is the King Charles' head of American historians; we can't get away from him. He is always there, and if he is not there as an influence, he is there as a counter influence. The contemporary historian has first to dispense with him before he can get on with the job, and that is not true of any other historian of our times. Beard is a great figure whose teachings and ideas and attitudes filter down from one generation of historians to another."

Symposium Program

Friday, October 11, 1974

3:00 p.m.   James L. Cooper, presiding
Associate Professor of History

Opening Remarks
William E. Kerstetter
President of the University

Eugene D. Genovese
Chairman, Department of History
University of Rochester
   "Charles A. Beard and the Economic
   Interpretation of History"

6:00 p.m.   Charles A. Beard Centennial Banquet
William E. Kerstetter, presiding

Detlev Vagts, speaker
Harvard University Law School
Grandson of Charles A. Beard

8:00 p.m.   Stanley Caine, presiding
Associate Professor of History

John Braeman
Professor of History
University of Nebraska
   "Charles A. Beard: Historian and
   Progressive"

Saturday, October 12, 1974

9:45 a.m.   John H. Wilson, presiding
Chairman, Department of History

Henry Steele Commager
Professor of History
Amherst College
    "Charles A. Beard: A Study in Paradox"

Panel Discussion

John J. Baughman, moderator
John Braeman
Henry S. Commager
Eugene D. Genovese
Clifton J. Phillips
Charles R. Tilden

A Grandson Remembers His Grandfather

Detlev Vagts

Mr. President, ladies and gentlemen. My first duty and pleasure is to thank all of you for being here, to thank those who came for miles and obviously prepared heavily and thoroughly in order to give the three addresses we have heard and are about to hear. Thanks to all the drivers, planners, adjusters of microphones and others without whom such a performance could not continue. I say, "Thank You," on behalf of myself and of my family. I know lawyers are always cautious about speaking for others where they have no direct and specific authority; some voice tells me that my grandfather is very pleased, too.

I know that he spoke often of this institution and that he felt that what he learned here did much to propel him onwards and forwards. I know that he went to DePauw University in the only way that one can really know that, I have a copy of the transcript, without which one is obviously not an educated man or woman, and I must say it is thrilling stuff: Oratory 4, Recent English and American Orators; English Literature 7, Carlyle and Tennyson. The

Detlev Vagts is Professor of Law at Harvard University and is a grandson of Charles and Mary Beard.

interesting thing is: the grade column is blank. Surely DePauw was not on Pass-Fail in those strenuous days! I understand there is a new law called the Buckley Amendment, under which a student can get copies of all data kept about him and I could perhaps demand it, the only trouble is that the statute says that the demand must be approved by the student's parents and that's going to be a little difficult to arrange at this late date. And while I speak of the thanks I ought also to say that I think my grandfather would have found particular pleasure in the kind gesture of Mr. Smith.* My grandfather felt that in the course of producing books, the total in sales of which was about 11,000,000 volumes, he made a substantial contribution to the good fortunes of the paper industry, and he would feel this was a just turnabout.

The fact that I, and not two people who are here who knew him better, am speaking, I suppose, is basically a function of a fact that when we got together I was the least able to say convincingly the standard words "Unaccustomed as I am to public speaking," and, since that's my profession, I shall try to do so.

A grandson's point of view on a grandfather is a somewhat special one. There is certainly more ignorance because the overlap of lives is much shorter than those of people on the next level, but there is certainly also a certain clarity of perspective, a certain distance of vision. One sees a grandfather without any of the complications which come from being the direct successor. Nobody has ever written learned volumes about grandfather complexes and I think the phenomenon is not existent.

I noted recently, with interest, another effort at describing or speaking about one's grandfather, this time

---

*During the Beard Centennial Dinner, Mr. J. Stanford Smith, member of the DePauw University Board of Trustees, announced that he desired to make a contribution towards the cost of the dinner.

from somebody who is professionally a refugee in the other direction. Stuart Hughes, whose grandfather was Charles Evans Hughes, describes him, I think, with admirable skill. I will at least purloin the title, it's irresistible: it's "They Don't Make Them Like That Any More." And I am sorry to say they don't! There is, of course, some difficulty in conveying to anybody under forty the concept of what Victorians were like (and Grandfather was a Victorian!). For one thing there is current a general conception that the striking thing about Victorians was how restricted, up-tight, they would now say, Victorians were. It's entirely true that in some narrow directions Grandfather was inhibited; although his contacts with agriculture and barns were extensive, he would have hesitated to use any of the barnyard language that now is common currency among students, male and female, which would have shocked him.

The thing that was really striking about Victorians in the flesh was their confidence and serenity and assurance — even about a man who, like my grandfather, spent most of his life questioning, putting, posing problems to people and to the discipline of history. There was an ultimate assurance that the game was worth playing, that the job was worth doing, and that a man could devote his life to pursuing it. This is something that one doesn't encounter too often nowadays. Somehow when I reach for analogies, similes, I think of trees, great, strong, spreading oaks under whose branches one could find calm and surcease from the storm. Stuart Hughes writes about the split in his grandfather, the way people misunderstood him as an individual because he was a public man, a man of affairs, a man whose robes and a beard concealed many elements of the real Hughes. My grandfather was not such a man, because it was in his professional life to be open and direct, to be himself with all people. With farmers, with people who came to take away the trash, students, visitors from abroad, he was one and the same. He was an outgoing man, but a man with a great deal of simplicity, despite the complexity of the life which he led those many years over many countries and continents.

But, again, the thing that one remembers is this sense of continuity and solidity. It was the things which he loved that I remember. There was his love of the land, of the soil. There are interesting speculations about my grandfather's relationships to his farm. The economic determinists assumed that he had carefully calculated that the rate of return reduced to present value of a farm would be superior to that available in the corporate market place. I wasn't old enough to make those calculations, but I doubt it. I think he had the farm because he loved it, because he felt that somebody cut off from the soil was no longer really safe and secure. There was always a feeling on his part that the people in Eastern establishment schools, who had not known the solidity of having one's own land under one's feet, really weren't all there. He loved the place on which he lived in the summers. He admitted quite frankly that he went out on the front porch when he first was shown it and he sat down and looked at the view. The view in those days was unspoiled Currier and Ives. The train used to go by and I can remember the steam whistle floating up from the valley. This would be the one note of industrialism for miles around, the big cheery whistle at the close of day. He looked out at this peaceful valley and he bought the place and then he turned around to see what else he had. He discovered he had what used to be a military academy and it took him some time to sell off the chapel, the lunch room and various other facilities. He also had a farm and for a while, two farms. He loved to go and see and loved to go and get the feel of the land, to talk to the farmer, to get a sense of how the farm was progressing. It comforted him to know that it was still there and that the plants came up every spring and that all was right on its course.

He felt deeply about the family. He would have loved the evidences of its continuity we have just heard this evening. He was concerned about his children, his grandchildren. He felt it important to tell them about his own grandparents, so that they might have a sense of the scale of history, the way that history is really just a stream of people in being. In 1937 he wrote me a note about his own family history. I'll just read a couple of paragraphs in which he recounts something—two episodes from the life of his own mother in this part of the world. At least it's so close that to an Easterner it seems like this part of the world.

> My own mother once told me a story of her youth. It seems that Grandfather had gone away over night perhaps to do some trading in a distant town. Late in the night a pack of wolves gathered about the cabin. The bolder ones came up to the heavy log cabin door and began to tear at it with their claws, howling like fiends! Grandmother was afraid they might manage to break the door down, so she pushed the children into a far corner of the cabin and kindled a pine knot in the fireplace. As soon as the knot was ablaze she unbarred the door and shoved the flaming brand into the faces and mouths of the wolves. As you may imagine, they did not like it. Thoroughly singed, the ring-leaders set off yelping and pawing their faces, and in a little while the others took the hint and fled too, leaving Grandmother and the children in peace.
>
> Another occasion in the night Grandmother heard a terrible noise in the small lean-to at the back of the cabin where foodstuffs were stored for the family use. After trying to make out what the whining and banging was, she peered into the room with the aid of a dim candle. And what did she see? A big black bear had smelled honey in a small keg, had staved in the top of the keg and thrust his shaggy head in to help himself. He tossed the keg round and round but could not get his head out. Grandmother grabbed an axe and finished Mr. Bruin off—which meant a fine bear rug for the floor and bear meat for the larder.

Well, people who talk about the future shock which hits our generation really ought to think about the changes that occurred within a relatively short space of time to people in the immediate preceding generation or two. Indiana certainly has changed, I saw nothing like that on the way here from the airport!

One of the strong, moving features of Grandfather's life was his love of this country, of the United States. Perhaps he would not frequently have used the phrase, although he knew it well, "The City on a Hill," because he thought of the United States as a great and noble experiment, something unique and to some degree exempt from the things that had gone wrong elsewhere. It gave him sorrow in the last years of his life to feel that things were going wrong and that America was becoming entangled in matters with which it could not sucessfully cope. I didn't at that time agree one by one with decisions he would have made, options he would have chosen, but one cannot but be conscious of what it is that we have lost by those decisions, necessary though they were. Many of the habits that we have taken on, things that we have learned to do abroad have come home: arbitrary patterns of governmental behaviour which he would have recognized as being alien to the American tradition that he loved, which we have let creep up on us in these last years. We are in the middle of a great crisis in which we are trying to determine whether America can clear itself of those toxins and return to being a country of simplicity and directness such as my grandfather would have wanted to hand on to his children and grandchildren and their children.

And finally, he loved his craft. He loved history, he thought it to be much more than a mere aggregation of facts and data. He loved the toughness of the material he had to wrestle with, the problems of arranging the myriad little facts into some sort of order that made sense. He loved, in the last analysis, the fact that it wasn't going to end, that it wasn't coming to some neat solution. He used to refer to a brief poem by the German poet, Heinrich Heine, which in translation says, "So let us keep on asking 'till finally someone comes with a handful of dirt and closes our mouths. Let us ask, 'Is that an answer, Is that an answer?' " And I sometimes think I still hear him asking that.

Eugene D. Genovese

After earning the Baccalaureate of Arts Degree at Brooklyn College in 1953, Mr. Genovese continued his education at Columbia University, receiving the M.A. degree in 1955 and the Ph.D. in 1959.

Prior to joining the University of Rochester faculty in 1969, Mr. Genovese served as Professor of History at the Polytechnic Institute of Brooklyn, Rutgers University, and Sir George Williams University (Montreal). His professional activities include membership on the editorial board of several journals, the executive council of the American Historical Association, and the program committee for the 1967 meeting of the Southern Historical Association in Atlanta. Presently, Mr. Genovese is chairman of the Department of History at the University of Rochester.

Among his publications are *The World the Slaveholders Made* and *Roll, Jordan, Roll.* In addition, he has edited and introduced six other texts and written numerous articles. Although his special interests are in South and Afro-American History, Mr. Genovese is well known as a Marxist analyst of American history in general.

Beard's Economic
Interpretation of History

Eugene D. Genovese

When I received President Kerstetter's gracious
invitation, I was simultaneously honored and startled:
honored, certainly, to be asked to participate in the
commemoration of one of America's giant historians; and
startled primarily because my occasional published
references to the work of Charles Beard have been rather
critical, although I hope not disrespectful or unapprecia-
tive, of his impressive accomplishments. But in truth, an
economic interpretation of history, more than any other,
has always provoked in me an urge to reach for a revolver,
and the scholars who invited me surely knew as much.

Since I could safely assume that my hosts had not lost
their minds and were not acting on masochistic impulses, I
have interpreted their invitation as a challenge to explore
the relationship between Beard's economic interpretation
and the Marxism with which it has often been confus-
ed--confused, I gather, much to Beard's irritation as
well as to the irritation of the Marxists. I shall, accordingly,
try to take a fresh look at Beard's economic interpretation
and to assess its strengths and weaknesses in a manner
that, I would hope, does justice to the integrity of his own
thought, rather than trying to squeeze it into the

framework of someone else's. The value of comparison with Marxian interpretation will, I hope, emerge solely from the light an alternative interpretation of history, which did after all influence Beard however slightly, may shed on his own splendid effort to combine a critical stance toward history with a strict respect for the facts. I shall try to avoid following the example of certain self-proclaimed "scientific" historians, whose appreciation and criticism of Beard has amounted to viewing his work as an interesting way station along the road to their own world-shaking theories.

With the exception of Turner and perhaps of Richard Hofstadter, no American historian of our century has exercised so pervasive an influence as Beard. The more that criticism and even expression of hostility pile up, the clearer becomes the extent of his intellectual hegemony — that is, the clearer it becomes that he asked the big questions and set the terms for much of the debate. Yet, his influence on recent Marxist historians has been slight. The flowering of Marxist history in America has come since about 1960: I refer especially to such outstanding and professionally respected work as that of Harold Woodman, Eric Foner, Ira Berlin, Robert Starobin, and somewhat less directly of Warren Susman and Christopher Lasch. Not that these and other Marxist scholars have failed to express respect and admiration for Beard as a historian — quite the contrary — but that is another matter.

Beard's work has, however, influenced profoundly the work of a parallel group of socialist historians — I refer to the followers of William Appleman Williams who have concerned themselves primarily with diplomatic history. And, indeed, I think it is largely to that group that the term "neo-Beardian" could most sensibly be applied. Williams himself is an original, whose complex thought has derived from many sources. Williams cannot simply be labeled as Beardian or Marxist, although both Beard and Marx influenced him deeply. What is plain is that most of the remarkable generation of revisionist scholars Williams taught or directly influenced have, for good reason, regarded Beard as a kind of intellectual grandfather. They, above all others, have worked in the spirit of Beard's early economic interpretation of foreign policy; and when one reflects on their success in introducing a new and vital approach to world affairs, one can only admire the power of Beard's own work—of the questions he asked and the hypotheses he brought to the surface. For, although most of these younger scholars became socialists, the underlying thrust of their historical interpretation has been if anything, economic-determinist in precisely the sense that some of the work of the early Beard might be so classed. With one or two exceptions, their work remains objectively anti-Marxist in precisely the same way as Beard's does. I think this point has been obscured simply because as socialists, they are political comrades of those of us who are Marxists, and because—if I may be frank—we are mostly good friends and do not want to cut each other up in public. The deeper philosophical antagonisms have therefore been hustled into the closet. As a result, it can be shown that much of the legitimate criticism now being leveled at that revisionist school—and I stress legitimate, in contradistinction to the vulgar political polemics to which they are being treated by resurrected Cold Warriors—represents a continuing and serious critique of Beard's own thought.

The revisionists have opened themselves to sharp attack by their inability to transcend Beardian categories, and they are now paying a high price for their unwillingness to ground their critique in a Marxian or alternative worldview. That is, they could avoid the difficulty by developing Beard's thought in an opposite direction and embracing a conservative ideology, variations of which are by no means incompatible with economic interpretation; but their socialist politics, not to mention sensibility, has blocked that road. Their present defensiveness, accordingly, exposes one of the major paradoxes of Beard's thought, which I want to explore today, and indeed one of the

paradoxes of every economic interpretation of history—
namely, that despite appearances it is philosophically
idealist to its core.

Beard's critics have often noted that he oscillated
between economic interpretation and economic determinism strictly defined, and sometimes perhaps he did, in
fact, confuse the two. I do think that this criticism has
some merit, but too much can be made of it. Beard, like
every serious historian, found out soon enough that the
human experience he was studying was too complex to fit
some grand deterministic formula. In his own way, he
recognized that a theory of history—that is, an attempt to
delineate the mainstream of social development—can at
best serve as a first approximation. The more interesting
problem lies elsewhere—in Beard's embrace of historical
relativism. First, let us recall with Hofstadter that it was the
mark of Beard's integrity and ruthless honesty that he
retreated from economic interpretation at the moment of
his greatest popularity—when his reputation was at its
summit. Men with less steady nerves or weaker
commitment to the search for truth would hardly have
indulged in public self-criticism at such a moment. In fact,
Beard's most effective early critic was probably Beard
himself. Thus, he set an example and a high standard for
those who came after him. Today, however, I wish to
consider his economic interpretation in its sharpest, early
forms in order to suggest that his retreat from it was in fact
built into the beginning—at least for a scholar as capable
as he was of self-criticism.

Beard's more superifical critics have sagely pondered
the apparent sommersault in which this exponent of a hard
economic materialism turned into a flaming idealist. They
do love to quote Beard's introduction to Bury's *Ideas of
Progress,* "Ideas, true and false, largely govern the world."
Beard's wiser critics, however, have properly sought the
roots of his later idealism in his apparent early
materialism. And at this point Marxists are entitled to
chuckle, for they have long held economic interpretation

to be a disguised form of philosophical idealism. Marx himself expressed impatience with those who sought to elevate any historical "factor" to the level of a prime mover. More to the point, as Marxists have long argued, concentration upon the economic factor in history cannot be sustained except as a concentration on the perceptions of economic interest—that is, on economic ideas in preference to other ideas. However many Marxists have themselves slipped into economic interpretation, the best have always regarded it as one variant of historical idealism. From this point of view, Beard's progression from economic interpretation to historical relativism was a logical development and reflected a stronger continuity in his thought than has generally been appreciated.

It is a commonplace of Beard criticism that he made enormous contributions to the study of interest-group politics but that he stumbled badly on cultural questions, despite I might add, his pioneering effort to take account of the totality of civilization. I should here suggest that Beard's well-known translation of "classes"—a term he used often—into interest groups prevented him from achieving that integrated human history to which he was committed. The same charge has been leveled at Marxist historians, but I should think that the work of Eric Hobsbawn and Christopher Hill alone constitutes an adequate refutation. On the contrary, Marxists have avoided the trap into which I fear Beard fell because they broke with the element of economic interpretation in Marx's thought, which was the very element Beard most admired.

A brief account of the Marxian alternative may, therefore, help us to understand the difficulties with which Beard struggled so tenaciously all his life. For Marxists, class relationships determine the contours, although certainly not the specifics, of historical development. Marxists define social classes in terms of relationships to the means of production—that is, to property. But in this sense, property means something other than what Beard meant; it means the primary categories of economic property, as distinguished by the broad character of the relationship to labor. It does not, that is, focus on specific forms of property within a given labor system—for example, on those categories as agricultural, industrial, or liquid capital which absorbed Beard's attention. Marx, whatever his faults, rarely fetishized historical problems. By defining social classes in relation to the means of production, he quite consciously defined them in relation to other classes. For him, the decisive questions concerned how flesh-and-blood human beings related to each other in the labor system.

Hence, Marxism is no more an economic interpretation of history than it is, say, a psychological interpretation, for social classes are viewed as the embodiment of the full range of human culture directly relevant to the politics of social process. Beard therefore knew what he was about when he scoffed at the idea that he himself was a Marxist and when he insisted that all he shared with Marx was a respect for the power of economic forces in history—a respect shared by many philosophers and historians, although of course in radically different ways. What I wish to insist upon, however, is that Beard, by taking a narrow view of this question, sealed himself off from an adequate historical psychology, among other aspects of culture.

I shall return to this price that Beard paid for his inability to come to terms with the pyschological dimension of history. For the moment, I wish merely to comment on the road he did not take by reflecting further on how Marxists as one alternative group have attacked this problem. For Marxists a social class embodies psychological patterns as well as discrete economic interests, for both reflect dialectically developing relationships of human beings to aggregates of other human beings as classes. Thus, unlike Beardian economic interpretation, which slides inexorably into behaviorist psychology—a psychology so unilluminating that Beard himself repeatedly abandoned it in order to return to strictly economic categories — a Marxian interpretation of history—that is, a class interpretation— has much more to gain from a Freudian psychology, despite its alleged idealism, than from a behaviorist psychology, despite its professed materialism, not to mention its official status in certain socialist countries. Freudian psychology, if I may pursue this for a moment, is, in its own terms, historical and developmental. And specifically, its central focus on the problem of authority, as conditioned by individual libidinal sublimation, expresses, in one aspect, a secularization of the theological problem of original sin; in the same way, it delineates the complex individual manifestations of the class problem of superordination and subordination in collective life.

Without room for a developmental psychology, Beard remained suspended between his own deep insights into interest-group politics and his life-long attempt to reconcile his powerful moral commitments with a narrow reading of the moral commitments of the historical figures he was writing about. I must therefore agree with Hofstadter's by no means unsympathetic comment that Beard, a man of high and admirable moral principles, nevertheless let his historical writing fall into considerable moral ambiguity. Hofstadter, among other fair-minded and respectful critics, proceeded to dismiss Beard's work in intellectual history as uninteresting and even embarrassing. I do think that Hofstadter's harsh judgment on *The American Spirit,* which he called "a dreary book", cannot easily be turned aside despite the merits of that book. And what can be said about Beard's discussion of Puritan theology, for example, which virtually dismisses that extraordinary cultural expression as a rationalization for people who did not want to pay taxes? Or consider, his analysis of the Nullification controversy as an expression of economic contention rather than of the slavery issue. William Freehling's brilliant book, *Prelude to Civil War,* which of course appeared long after Beard's death, buried that argument. But during Beard's lifetime the essential point of Freehling's critique had been suggested by many others, and Beard was well aware of it. He nevertheless pressed his own point relentlessly. If, he argued, southerners had yielded on economic issues, then the North probably would have allowed them their state-rights doctrines and what I fear he considered assorted other trivia. For him, throughout his valuable and indeed path-breaking reflections on what he so suggestively called "the second American revolution," only the clash of economic interests proved irreconcilable. Some critics have therefore argued that Beard could not account for the moral, and ultimately the political, power of the abolitionists and had to quantify them out of existence. What those critics have not stressed is that implicit in Beard's interpretation of this and other questions is a social psychology that has men acting in accordance with perceived interests and specifically economic interests. Before long, he is led to treat much, if not all ideology, including religion and philosophy, as largely reflexes of economic interest. For example, he treats antebellum southern state-rights and constitutional theory as a rationalization of the economic interests of the cotton planters. I doubt that many historians would today credit this contemptuous dismissal of the very heart of southern political culture. It never seems to have occurred to him to seek the social origins of the southern constitutional argument in the plantation-slave regime, which inherently projected a powerful resistance to centralized state power, quite apart from any economic specifics.

It is on this recurring and vital level of historical analysis that Beard's fascination with economic interest groups committed him to a superficial psychology, which weakened some of his finest and most enduring efforts. And if I may drive this point home: It is precisely here that Beard's reduction of Marxism to one more variant of economic interpretation cost him dearly. For Marxists, whose social psychology derives primarily from Hegel's *Phenomenology of Mind,* the decisive starting-point for an analysis of historical motivation is the development of social class relations. Thus, a Marxist who wanted to understand the southern temper and the psychological wellsprings of southern political action would look not to the configuration of economic interests, although he certainly would not ignore them, but to the dialectics of the master-slave relationship itself—a subject Beard, I think for good reasons, did not touch. Yet the great pity is that long before all except the great Dr. W.E.B. DuBois and a very few other American historians, Beard took social history seriously: he looked at women, the family, the daily life of the working classes, when few if any other historians were willing to do so. Without a theory of social process and an appropriate psychology, however, the splendid discussions of social life in his work and that of Mary Beard do not shed full light on those political developments which must remain at the center of any meaningful interpretation of history.

Perhaps the most striking feature of Beard's economic interpretation, even at its strongest point, is the very absence either of a general theory of historical development or of a consistent economic theory. No one has put this problem better or more succinctly than Mr. Commager in one brilliant sentence on the reception of the *Economic Interpretation of the Constitution* and the *Economic Origins of Jeffersonian Democracy:* "If these interpretations were open to criticism, it was not so much because they assigned to economics a decisive place in history as because they excluded history from a controlling place in economics." And if I may say so, it was V.I. Lenin who made the point much more rudely by demonstrating that in the game of "historical factors" politics is, if anything, more important than economics, for politics— which Mao Tse-Tung defined harshly but not unfairly as command of the gun—can reshape the economy at least as thoroughly and even more quickly than economics can reshape politics. Beard was a man who knew a great deal about the world. He probably did not need Lenin to teach him that lesson, and he certainly drew his own conclusions from the Russian Revolution. In any case, his economic interpretations did not add up to a general interpretation of history, nor did he want them to; more strikingly, neither did they project a theory of economic development.

And here again I shall ask you to bear with me if I compare him with Marx. Marxian political economy centers on a struggle for control of society's economic surplus. Under capitalism, this becomes a struggle for control of surplus-value, but other modes of production, such as ancient slavery or medieval seigneurialism, had their analogues, which amount to what Marx called "the law of motion" in historical process. Beard's rejection of this part of Marx's thought—that is, his rejection of everything distinctive and essential in Marxism—resulted neither from ignorance nor from confusion. Rather, Beard's sympathy for democratic collectivism and his respect for English Fabianism never overcame, as Hofstadter so cogently argued, his fundamental commitment to a bourgeois social order—an order, I might add, he fought so long himself to humanize. Hofstadter has drawn attention to Beard's critique of industrialism as a critique of waste, of competitive excesses, and of an ultimate dehumanization—a critique that by-passed the class nature of the capitalist social system as a whole. A similar critique could be made of Hofstadter, but that is not our problem today.

Beard's politics were his own business; and E.R.A. Seligman, who influenced him, was right to argue that an economic interpretation of history logically does not commit a man to socialism. Indeed, sometimes I think the most fanatical believers in extreme economic determinism are to be found among big businessmen and conservative economists. But the essential ingredient in Marxism, in sharp contrast to those economic interpretations it superficially resembles, is not merely a recognition of classes but of the centrality of class struggle. Beard himself did speak of class struggle, although he defined it in a very different way. For Marx, class struggle rests on an expropriation of a social surplus produced by labor—that is, on exploitation. Now, even a theory of exploitation cannot compel allegiance to socialism, but it does establish a powerful moral tendency in that direction. Beard had too great an intelligence not to anticipate the problem, and too much integrity to fudge it. It was no accident that he spoke of classes but in practice defined them as interest groups within classes. Unlike those who accused Beard of confusion and sloppiness here, I should suggest that he was struggling to avoid being dragged down a road he knew his temperament and notions of political morality forbade him to travel. He therefore fell back on an economic skepticism that, as Mr. Commager remarked, sacrificed the historical dimension of economics and eventually led him to relativism.

Beard's laudable refusal to pursue metahistory simultaneously led him to reject, from the very beginning of his economic explorations, the central concern of a class interpretation of history—namely, a concern, which need not be metahistorical, with the dynamics of history as process. His unwillingness to commit himself to a particular school of economic theory, whether bourgeois or Marxist, represented therefore one facet of this larger agnosticism.

From a Marxist point of view, this paradox of an economic interpretation of history without a dominant economic theory and without a theory of historical process represents the inevitable outcome of the idealist foundations of all economic interpretation and of the attendant refusal to view economics itself as a historical process.

Beard's uncertainty with economic theory hardly arose from ignorance, for his work shows that he read deeply in the literature of the contending schools. But uncertainty it was, as is most clearly revealed in his book *The Idea of National Interest*. The influence of English left-liberalism and Fabianism appears sharply in his virtual identification of commercial expansion and overseas markets with imperialism. He criticizes the theory of free trade's ostensible mutual advantages by invoking ideas reminiscent of Marx and especially of Lenin: he cites the uneven development of nations within the worldwide "mode of production." That term certainly derives primarily from Marx, although Beard's definition was implicitly quite different. Nevertheless, a critique of commerce and overseas markets as *ipso facto* imperialist makes no sense except on the economic theory of "super-profits"—that is, an economic theory that accounts for the extraction of a rate of profit well in excess of the national average. There are, of course, theories other than Marxian that try to account for super-profits, but like Lenin's, these theories—Gunnar Myrdal's for example—end with the politics of class rule in national form anyway. Precisely at that point Beard turned, implicitly at least, to a political economy akin to that of J.A. Hobson, which stresses the parasitism and greed of specific economic interests rather than the class exigencies of capitalism as a whole. Unlike Hobson, Beard had too firm a grasp of world politics to remain confortable with this formulation; he suggested that the ruling class, and he was speaking specifically of the United States, normally unites to defend the foreign interests of any of its sectors. Moreover, quite suddenly (p. 118) he attacks what he calls the "profit economy" and its lack of any ruling philosophy other than one of profit maximization. He writes of "a swollen pool of liquid capital...pressing its banks for profitable outlets—anywhere in the world." And he comes close to judging international capitalism as an anarchic system of production devastated by the uneven development of its national sectors. In all this, he approximates Marxism more closely than anywhere else in his work, so far as I can see. He never settles scores with Marx, with Lenin, or with Hobson. When he ends by lamenting the lack of an adequate balance sheet to reveal the relationship between the costs and profits of imperialism, he in effect retreats to Hobson's ground. My criticism here is not that, wittingly or not, Beard chose a version of Hobson's economics over that of Marx and Lenin—which would have been his privilege—but that in fact he did not consistently commit himself to any economic theory at all. Hence, he ended in an eclecticism that drew indiscriminately on contending and irreconcilable schools of political economy and that introduced an often-noted ambiguity into his work, which opened him to attack for his powerful and still important critique of American foreign policy. His critics, fairly and unfairly, have had a field day with these inconsistencies, and they are now scoring heavily against those revisionist diplomatic historians who seek to construct an economic interpretation of foreign policy without an economic theory to explain the explanations. These neo-Beardians, therefore, usually end where Beard did, instead of developing his thought creatively. For all their pages devoted to economics, what often emerges is an account of how members of the ruling class perceive their economic interests. What does not emerge is a coherent critique of the economic process itself and of the objective validity of those perceptions. Now it makes a great deal of difference whether people in command of policy are perceiving their interests on the basis of an analysis that corresponds to objective reality or whether they have been misled into a series of strategic estimates that do not conform to objective reality. But this is the kind of a question with which economic interpretations of history have great difficulty.

Thus, there is an organic relationship between Beard's unwillingness to raise his economic interpretation to a general theory of historical development, his eclectic and uncertain use of economic theory, and his ambiguous critique of imperialism. The result of this configuration was a retreat into historical idealism characterized not so much by his later relativism as by his initial focus on the politics of discrete interest groups.

One of Beard's great contributions to American history was to come to terms with the challenge of Turner's inward view of American history and yet relate it to the sweep of Western civilization as a whole. In so doing, he bequeathed a messier package than Turner did and he risked much greater inconsistency; but, as in so many other respects, he simultaneously forced a confrontation with the major questions that continue to haunt us. The specifics of his assessments of European history in relation to American nonetheless do raise problems inherent in his customary identification of social classes and economic interest groups—an identification that in fact transforms the professed focus on classes into a classless view of social process by locating social conflict within a given propertied class rather than between classes.

Beard's much-criticized view of personalty versus realty in the constitutional debate or his projection of a struggle between capitalism and agrarianism in much of American history flowed from a more general view of the sweep of European and American history. When, for example, Beard interprets Machiavelli as urging the Prince to balance the claims and power of the contending classes, he is turning away from a possible class interpretation of Machiavelli's thoughts on state power. But more to the point, Beard proceeds to applaud Locke for understanding that the state exists primarily to protect property rights. What Beard does not do is to explore the nature of the property in question. He thus interprets the transformation of Central Europe, specifically Austria, as reflecting changes within the nobility, the class nature of which he never addresses. Beard never analyzes the significance of changes in the forms of property from seigneurial to bourgeois and therefore never addresses the decisive question of the metamorphosis of the landed classes, both the ruling and the ruled, from one social type to another.

This silence reflected neither oversight nor lapse in judgment. It paralleled his discussion of early modern English history as abstracted from the transformation in property relations there. In this way, he opened himself to the later attack of such diverse consensus historians as Boorstin, Hartz, and Hofstadter, who quite properly insisted that America had inherited a bourgeois social system and attendant system of political ideals. Since Beard's reduction of a class analysis to interest-group analysis appeared nowhere so sharply as in his slighting of the slavery question, he surrendered in advance his best counter-argument—the one suggested by his notion of a "second American revolution", which might, if he had carried it further, have demolished almost single-handedly so much of the consensus interpretation of American history.

Beard thereupon, as his consensus critics have cogently argued, proceeded to exaggerate the sharpness of the quarrels over the Constitution and the shape of the early republic and to fall into the error of viewing the agrarian reactions against commercial and industrial policies and excesses as evidence of class struggle. Had Beard really meant classes when he wrote of classes, he would have had to confront the American farmers, who after all arose within a bourgeois not a seigneurial social system, as an agrarian manifestation of a single process of capitalist development, much as Hofstadter was later to do within his own ideological framework.

Beard's difficulty in sustaining a capitalist-agrarian dichotomy has been ably, as well as not-so-ably criticized from many points of view. Accordingly, I should like to restrict myself to one aspect, which may illustrate the dangers of trying to do without a theory of economic development. Beard himself noted that the party of Jefferson and Jackson, which he identified as agrarian, rose to power in 1800 and held power until 1861, except for two brief quirks in 1840 and 1848. He also noted, but could not satisfactorily explain, Jefferson's acceptance of the capitalist program of his predecessors and the steady consolidation of capitalist power under a long line of ostensibly agrarian presidents. Now, if economics controls politics and if capitalism and something called agrarianism are an antagonistic, none of this is readily explicable. This anomaly, at the least, challenged Beard to lay out a theory to account for so irresistible an economic process.

By avoiding that challenge, or at least not giving it his full attention, Beard was able to avoid what might have been the greatest embarrassment in two of his greatest and most lasting books, *Economic Origins of Jeffersonian Democracy* and the *Rise of American Civilization.* The embarrassment to which I refer concerned the South and the slaveholders' regime. Specifically, it concerned his sound appraisal of the Jefferson-Jackson party as a coalition of slaveholders and free farmers; his recognition that the coalition was ultimately unstable; and his hopeless attempt to seek the source of division in narrowly defined economic interests. I shall here have to settle for one observation on Jefferson's and Jackson's economic programs—their support for territorial expansion and the rapid development of the West. The outcome of that so-called agrarian anti-capitalist movement was in fact the rapid creation of the greatest home market for capitalist industry in world history. Indeed, if one wanted to argue that Jefferson, not Hamilton, deserves to be considered the father of American capitalist development, he could make his case with at least as much economic logic as could a Hamiltonian.

In short, Beard's economic interpretation rested on a repudiation of a theory of economic development—that is, of capitalist development—and on a repudiation of political economy in general. Nothing so clearly betrays the idealism of his early thought and so clearly establishes the link between his apparently materialist economic interpretation and his later relativism. That his work, including his best and most admirable, was plagued by an almost Manichean view of social conflict—despite his frequent denials—therefore need surprise no one.

At this juncture we confront the inability of Beard's economic interpretation to account for the collapse of the alliance between western farmers and southern slave-holders. Yet in the same works, Beard shed much light on the strictly economic aspect of the collapse of that alliance. Beard's concern with "civilization", not merely the economy, might have drawn his attention more sharply to the cultural divergence that accompanied the economic and that accounted for so much of the violent tenor of antebellum life. But here again, Beard could construct no adequate psychology of contending interest groups. Even when he spoke most firmly of classes rooted in property relations, he quickly made plain that he meant such entities as manufacturers, merchants, and bond-holders; and in fact, even when he spoke of the landed interest, if we put the planters aside, he usually spelled out a class of essentially capitalist and petty-capitalist farmers. No wonder, then, that he tended to reduce political psychology, as well as ideology, to a simple reflex of economic interests. No sensible developmental historical psychology could be built on a theory of interest groups. Beard's implicit rejection of Freud was therefore of a piece of his rejection of Marx. Taken as a piece, he cut himself off from that focus on the historical development of social relations which might have led to a materalist rather than idealist development of his early thought.

And it might have saved him from what some critics have called his misreading of Madison's political theory—which I fear was in fact the very political theory on which he pegged so much of his early economic interpretation. For Beard paraphrased Madison as follows: "The latent causes of faction are thus sown in the nature of man..."; but Beard then proceeded to a startling *nonsequitur,* "Thus, in the opinion of the Father of the Constitution, politics springs inevitably, relentlessly out of economics." I should have thought that Madison was saying something different—that politics and economics alike spring from a human nature marked by inequality of faculties and haunted by what Christian theologians call original sin and what Freudians call an aggressive instinct.

One would think, that is, that Madison, in his own terms was alluding to the psychological manifestations of the contradictions inherent in the nature of men as autonomous wills and yet as dependent upon the repressions demanded by the needs of society. Beard certainly did not intend to distort Madison's views; rather, he seems to have been making an effort to assimilate those views to his own interpretation in a way he certainly considered responsible. But no economic interpretation of history can be rendered flexible enough to account for that dimension of human experience, although a class interpretation can, for it views the class struggle as a social terrain on which warring tendencies are fought out in collective form.

When Beard repeatedly dismissed ideological issues as abstractions that mask material interests, he deduced sensibly from his focus on interest groups. The deeper questions of social relations, in contradistinction to market or other purely economic relations, certainly troubled him, but did not engage his full attention. It was therefore easy for him, and is easy for neo-Beardians, to suggest that American commitments abroad and the attendant risks of war would probably rise and fall in rough proportion to investments and direct economic stakes. Beard advanced this thought as a hypothesis and never as a dogma, although some recent writers have made it into dogma. From this point of view, the Vietnam War—to take a recent example—becomes inexplicable, despite some dubious recent attempts at economic interpretation. The point of view cannot adequately account for the commitment to a national policy of defense of a world-wide social system, specifically manifested in a deep ideological and psychological opposition to the expansion of communism regardless of direct economic involvement.

Beard seemed troubled by these difficulties and eventually made some valiant attempts to work out of them. In his thought-provoking introduction to Bury's

Idea of Progress, as well as elsewhere, he provides a good many valuable insights into the role of technology in the modern world and in particular explores the possibility that a certain development of the productive forces of society would lay the basis for a new era of freedom by liberating man's consciousness from enslavement to mere interest. It is perhaps enough to note that even if we accept Beard's argument as a sound evaluation of the thrust of present forces, it would only underscore his inability to reconcile economic with cultural, and objective with subjective, forces in historical process.

Ironically, Beard's greatest success in applying an economic interpretation of history came in the very work for which he has been most thoroughly criticized and attacked. Much valid criticism notwithstanding, Beard did shed light on the origins of the Constitution and the making of early American democracy. Forrest McDonald has corrected empirical errors and produced a more balanced view, but McDonald's debt to Beard's questions and categories can hardly be missed. And if others, like Hofstadter himself, have succeeded in shifting the terms of the debate, they too have clearly built on Beard's foundation and have had to forge their own viewpoint in a prolonged argument with his tenacious theses and insights. They have not so much refuted as transcended his work. Hofstadter's ability to do so was particularly interesting—putting aside his extraordinary personal talents—because it flowed in part from his own insight into the heart of Beard's difficulties with the class question. Hofstadter knew his Marxism well, first as a youthful, brief adherent, and then as a profound antagonist; he based his own work on the sound judgment that the only class struggle at issue pitted the slaveholders against the capitalists, including the petty-capitalist farmers and that the struggles between interest groups were being fought out within a consensus based on adherence to bourgeois social relations and property ownership.

Beard is therefore entitled to the last laugh. If Hofstadter, and Beard's other critics, are right on this major point, then, except for the secession crisis, American politics can best be studied as a series of sharp antagonisms within a class consensus. If so, Beard's focus on economic interests may have led him into exaggerations and errors, but no one could seriously doubt that the economic conflicts, to which he drew attention, have played at least as great and probably a greater role than any other in the specifics of our political history. In fact, when all is said and done, the consensus framework itself, by projecting ideological unity based on a single property system, returns to Beard's ground and magnifies precisely the conflicts within that consensus—conflicts that have pitted competing economic interests against each other. For this reason alone—although there are certainly others—Beard's books continue to help shape a vigorous debate.

If I have emphasized the critical side, I have done so in the spirit of Beard's relentless demand for reappraisal. We have so thoroughly absorbed his accomplishments that we can easily forget how much we owe him. Criticism of what may be perceived as his failures cannot diminish his stature as a man who so clearly reoriented the study of American history. Indeed, when we reflect on the depth and breadth of his impact—on the extent to which he asked the big questions with which we still grapple and on the extent to which he liberated American history from so much cant and trivia, I think we may say of him what he himself once said of Buckle. Beard admired Buckle's achievement and critical spirit but in the end found his specific theses wanting. In summary, Beard wrote of Buckle, "Yet, conceivably it might be better to be wrecked on an express train bound to a destination than to moulder in a freight car sidetracked in a well-fenced lumber yard." Beard, too, was an express train.

John Braeman

A native of New York City, Mr. Braeman earned his baccalaureate degree magna cum laude from Harvard College in 1954, and completed the Ph.D. degree at Johns Hopkins University in 1960.

In addition to the University of Nebraska, where he has served as Professor of History since 1965, Mr. Braeman taught previously at Ohio State University and Brooklyn College. His research and teaching are concerned primarily with 20th century American history.

He is a member of Phi Beta Kappa, the Organization of American Historians, and a member of the editorial board of "American Studies".

Mr. Braeman is author of a biography of a distinguised DePauw alumnus entitled *Albert J. Beveridge: American Nationalist,* published by the University of Chicago Press in 1971. He is also the editor of a series of volumes entitled *Modern America* published by the Ohio State University Press.

Charles A. Beard:
Historian and Progressive

John Braeman

During his life, as after his death, Charles A. Beard evoked widely differing reactions. An unsympathetic Allan Nevins dismissed him as the exponent of "a smart, hard materialism." His former student and long-time friend Raymond Moley regarded him as the exemplar of a "hard-bitten realism": a realism heavily laced with skepticism toward "orthodoxy—even his own earlier orthodoxies." His "real spirit," the "essential 'style' of the man," his friend and neighbor Matthew Josephson wrote, "was realistic, skeptical, pragmatic."[1]

Beard himself took as his guiding principle "to look at things coldly and realistically, rather than through the rosy spectacles of some dogmas satisfactory to inherited preconceptions." Throughout his life, he expressed his scorn for sentimental do-gooders out of touch with the hard realities of the world. "Aspiration without knowledge," he warned a 1939 Symposium on Some Contemporary Realities, "can merely make trouble and sorrow in the world." And in his disillusionment after World War II, his most withering contempt was reserved for "idealists." "Praised be the idealists," he exclaimed. "By comparison the Press is holy!"[2]

There was a streak of the gadfly, the irreverent, the iconoclast in Beard, a delight in deflating pretensions, in startling his audience, in puncturing the conventional wisdom. His talent as a satirist would at times lead him into exaggeration, even caricature. He once told his class that the very best equipment of the scholar was to consider at all times that the very opposite of accepted faith may be true.[3]   Beard's commitment to what he called "the Socratic elenchus"—"new facts...constantly challenging old mental patterns and imagery"[4] —was a life-long passion. "When I come to the end," he said in a mood of self-reflection, "my mind will still be beating its wings against the bars of thought's prison."[5]

Yet there was another side to Beard. His distinguished fellow historian Carl L. Becker glimpsed the dual nature of Beard's personality when he called him a "hard-headed idealist" who was simultaneously "an exasperated cynic and a warm-hearted friend of suffering humanity"—"too sophisticated not to delight in dispelling illusions; yet too humanely sympathetic to fall back into the easy cynicism of one who is content merely to observe the tragic comedy of existence." The philosopher Irwin Edman, who took Beard's course in American government while a freshman at Columbia, recalled how he conveyed to his students not simply his "passionate concern" for "understanding the realities of government," but his "ideal of government: the liberation of the energies of men." "We work the whole time," Mary Beard confided to a friend, "...because we want to know and say what we think we know...to help the human race to realize its highest potentialities."[6]

Beard, an admirer wrote, "had a deep concern about human beings, a profound respect for human dignity."[7] Nor did he limit humanity to its male half. Recalling his grandmother's activities as the neighborhood angel of mercy, he belabored historians of the frontier for their failure to give sufficient weight to the civilizing role of women in subduing the wilderness.[8] He was insistent upon giving his wife, Mary, full recognition as his collaborator on many of his most important works; he encouraged her in her own efforts to remedy the neglect of women's role in history by male historians.[9] He himself was an active supporter of women's rights—not simply the right to vote, but the larger right to the fullest possible self-development.[10]

Throughout his life, Beard's overriding commitment was to the fulfillment of "the promise of American life." The indispensable prerequisite was material abundance for all—" a high standard of life for the whole mass of the American people."[11] But material abundance was simply the means to the larger end of a fuller, freer, and happier life. In the depths of the Great Depression, Beard wrote rhapsodically about the America of his dreams: a land "without the degradation of poverty and unemployment on the one side or the degradation of luxury, rivalry, and conspicuous waste on the other...a beautiful country—homes beautiful; communities and farms beautiful; stores and workshops beautiful." "Sheer utopianism, my masters will say," he admitted. But "without vision men and women perish, nations perish."[12]

There was in Beard a continuing tension between the scholar and the activist. During his years at Columbia, he was a highly popular and successful teacher as well as an extraordinarily productive scholar. But he felt a growing restiveness within the academy.[13] His resignation in 1917 was a disinterested and noble protest against what he saw as intolerable violations of academic freedom. At the same time, his departure had its aspect of personal release. "It is certainly a relief," he confessed to Albert J. Beveridge, "to be out of Mr. Butler's asylum!"[14] There were in university life, he complained a decade after his resignation, too many hindrances to "creative thinking in politics"—"too much routine, not enough peace; too much calm, not enough passion;...too many books, not enough strife of experience; too many students, not enough seekers...

above all too many sacred traditions that must be conserved." [15]

Yet he himself recognized his temperamental unsuitability for political activism. He was too much the individualist, too much his own man, too much the iconoclast to be a party loyalist. He left his father's party, the G.O.P., in 1900 over imperialism and thereafter remained a political free lance.[16] He was even chary of lending his name to causes or committees. "Merely to sanction undertakings in which I have no expertness," he wrote turning down F.D.R.'s proffered appointment to the commission to celebrate the sesquicentennial of the adoption of the Constitution, "is contrary to my conception of personal responsibility." "In sheer self-defense—to get a little time for study," he explained in refusing an invitation to join the Committee for the Defense of Leon Trotsky, "I am compelled to adhere to a simple rule: Don't underwrite committees (for they may do anything) and stick to matters of which I have some personal knowledge." [17]

Beard's resolution of the tension—to promote reform through his scholarship and writing—rested upon his faith in man's basic rationality and his belief that the people if properly informed would act wisely and justly. This faith underlay his support for such progressive era reforms as the initiative, referendum, and recall;[18] his reports and surveys for the New York Bureau of Municipal Research; [19] and his own efforts in later years to set forth "the intellectual and moral qualities that Americans have deemed necessary to civilization in the United States." [20]

His commitment to preserving the free market place of ideas inspired Beard's life-long championship of civil liberties. While still at Columbia, he brought down upon himself the wrath of the local press and the Columbia trustees when he spoke out against demands that radical speakers be barred from the public schools because one had reportedly declared "To hell with the American flag." "We could not expect to have liberty without some abuse of it," he explained, and "as between having too much authority or too much liberty, I preferred the latter." [21] In the years that followed, he stood up against the vigilantism of the superpatriots during World War I, denounced the notorious Lusk Committee of the New York state legislature during the postwar Red Scare, attacked the State Department's gag prohibiting exiled former Hungarian premier Count Michael Karolyi from speaking on politics, spoke out against F.B.I. chief J. Edgar Hoover's subversive-hunting, and protested the proposed Nixon-Mundt bill during the McCarthy era. [22] All progress, he affirmed in his presidential address before the American Political Science Association, depends upon "the widest freedom to inquire and expound....It is in silence, denial, evasion, and suppression that danger really lies, not in open and free analysis and discussion. Surely if any political lesson is taught by the marvelous history of English-speaking peoples it is this." [23]

Despite his own disillusionment with academic life, Beard had an abiding faith in the importance of education in a democracy: a faith that underlay his role in the founding of the New School for Social Research and the Workers Education Bureau of America, his long-time involvement with the American Association for Adult Education, his service on the Commissions on the Social Studies of the American Historical Association and the Department of Superintendence of the National Education Association, his part in drafting the 1937 report of the N.E.A.'s Educational Policies Commission on *The Unique Function of Education in American Democracy*, and his ties with the social reconstructionist group of educators centered around the journal *The Social Frontier* during the 1930's. [24]

Yet Beard was ambivalent about what exactly the function of education should be—an ambivalence that reflected his own inner conflict between scholarship and reform. Ideally education should aim at "the liberation of intelligence," should "encourage the remorseless use of the Socratic elenchus." [25] In practice, he wished education to inculcate those values which he himself felt deeply about. Thus, in the controversial final report he wrote for the A.H.A.'s Commission on the Social Studies, he called upon educators to prepare students for the "new age of collectivism [that] is emerging.[26] And as he became more and more worried about what he saw as threats to historic American values and institutions, the more loudly he called for education that would instill in students knowledge of and respect for this country's distinctive and unique heritage.[27]

At the same time, Beard stood up steadfastly and forthrightly in defense of academic freedom. Despite his own support for American entry into World War I, he resigned his Columbia position in protest against the dismissal of anti-war colleagues.[28] He called for a full investigation of the firing in 1936 of Yale Divinity School professor Jerome Davis allegedly for his pro-Soviet views.[29] He spearheaded the campaign that led the University of Minnesota Board of Regents in 1938 to reinstate William A. Schaper, who had been fired during the World War I hysteria, as professor emeritus of political science. [30] When the Hearst newspapers undertook a campaign against supposed Communist infiltration in colleges and schools, he came to the National Education Association's Atlantic City convention in February, 1935 and denounced the publisher as "an enemy of everything that is noblest and best in our American tradition." His intervention played a major role in blocking Hearst's efforts to win N.E.A. backing for his red-hunt. "We baffled Hearst at Atlantic City in 1935," he reported proudly to F.D.R., "and overwhelmed him at St. Louis in February, 1936."[31]

Beard's ambition to use scholarship for reform purposes drew his interest first to political science. In his writings on politics, Beard was part of the larger "revolt against formalism" underway during the progressive era.[32] His aim, he explained to the publisher of his projected textbook on American government, was to look beneath abstractions "to the great problem of how things are actually done." This same concern to show "how things actually were run" underlay his effectiveness and popularity as a teacher.[33] In his 1908 Columbia lecture on *Politics*, Beard expounded the group basis of politics. And he went on to assert—most strikingly in his landmark *An Economic Interpretation of the Constitution of the United States* (1913)—the primacy of economic interests in shaping men's political ideas and behavior.[34]

Like his fellow rebels against formalism, Beard was influenced by Darwinism. Since life is change, the present had to be explained historically. At the same time, history was for Beard not simply a tool of analysis. The past, he and his colleague James Harvey Robinson declared in the 1907 text, *The Development of Modern Europe*, should be "consistently subordinated" to the interests of the present.[35] History could—and should—illuminate the roots and sources of modern-day problems. Beard shared Robinson's faith in history as an intellectual catharsis that would liberate men from the burden of myth, tradition, and obsolete ideas. But he went even further and claimed that history, properly written, could provide guidelines for the future. The historian, he declared in 1919, "endures only in so far as he succeeds in casting through the warp of the past the weft of the future—the future which he can behold only by prophetic discernment." "It is given to but a few to walk with the gods in the dusk of ages"[36] —and his ambition was to join that select body.

In his youthful optimism, Beard had no doubt that the historical process was moving inexorably forward. The theme of his first book—*The Industrial Revolution*, published in 1901, during his involvement with the Ruskin Hall workers' education movement—was full of praise for technological advances and the scientific method for bettering the lot of mankind and paving "the way to higher forms of industrial methods in which the people, instead of a few capitalists, will reap the benefits." "The central theme of history" he wrote—and the hallmark of "modern times"—was man's "progressive" realization of his "right and power...corporately to control every form of his material environment." [37]

Like so many reformers of his generation, Beard extolled the gains made in expanding the functions of municipal government to deal with the problems of an increasingly urbanized society. Yet he realized that the larger, more "fundamental" problems facing the country could be dealt with only at the national level.[38] The difficulty was, he explained in his 1914 book on *Contemporary American History*, "the lack of correspondence between the political system and the economic system." Despite the rise of "a national system of manufacturing, transportation, capital, and organized labor," the federal government remained "powerless...to regulate...nearly all of the great national interests." [39]

Beard shared contemporary reformers' unhappiness over the prevailing judicial interpretation of the Constitution that appeared to present an insuperable barrier to federal regulation of economic life. "Isn't most of the stuff given forth by standpat lawyers on the mystery and sanctity of the judiciary too comical for words," he exclaimed to Arthur M. Schlesinger. "Nearly every time the court has set aside a federal act of importance," he told Albert J. Beveridge, "the court has been wrong, and reversed by the judgment of history." [40] He even set out—or, at least, so Raymond Moley recalled—in writing his 1912 study on *The Supreme Court and the Constitution* to prove that John Marshall and the Court had wrongly usurped the power of judicial review. But his study of the evidence led him to conclude that "the leading members of the Convention...believed that the judicial power included the right and duty of passing upon the constitutionality of acts of Congress." [41]

In this work, Beard linked "the intention of the framers of the Constitution to establish judicial control of legislation" with their anxiety "above everything else to safeguard the rights of private property against any levelling tendencies on the part of the propertyless masses." [42]   He made this motive of the Founding Fathers the theme of his

controversial book on the framing and adoption of the
Constitution published the following year. Beard's motives
in writing *An Economic Interpretation of the Constitution*
remain unclear. He had a deep respect and admiration for
the framers' wisdom and realism, and he was surprised,
even hurt, by the hostile reaction to his work.[43] In his
preface, he indicated that his aim was simply "to suggest
new lines of historical research." And he explicitly denied
in his introduction to the 1935 edition that the work had
been "written with reference to immediate controversies." [44]

But those "immediate controversies" inevitably shaped
reactions to the book. His conclusion that the Constitution
was the work of the propertied few designed to safeguard
the economic interests of their class against popular
majorities was sufficient to upset embattled conservatives;
his intimations that the framers had sought to line their
own pockets by enhancing the value of the government
securities they held added insult to injury. "Scavengers,
Hyena-Like, Desecrate the Graves of the Dead Patriots We
Revere," screamed the headline in Warren G. Harding's
Marion Star. [45] Conversely, reformers hailed Beard's
findings as removing a major intellectual obstacle to their
program of federal government action to regulate business
and assist the less favored members of American society.
Given "an undemocratic Constitution...'put over'
by a small minority of able, vigorous and unscrupulous
personal property owners," Herbert Croly (drawing upon
Beard) wrote in *Progressive Democracy*, the "path of
progressive democratic fulfillment" lay in making "the
Constitution alterable at the demand and according to the
dictates of a preponderant prevailing public opinion." [46]
Beard himself drew up for a group of social reformers a
proposed method for easier amendment to bring the
Constitution "under the control of the people." [47]

Beard followed his study of the adoption of the Constitution with his *Economic Origins of Jeffersonian Democ-*

racy. Taking his lead from Frederick Jackson Turner, he pictured the battle between Hamilton and Jefferson as a continuation of the struggle over the Constitution—"A conflict between capitalistic and agrarian interests." Although his sympathies appeared—at least, super-ficially—to lie with Jefferson and his followers, Beard was painfully aware of the limitations of the Jeffersonian legacy. Jefferson himself had made his peace with "the capitalistic interests."[48] More importantly, the placid agrarian world of Jefferson was irrevocably gone—and Jeffersonian limited government dogmas were not merely irrelevant, but a liability. Beard stood ideologically closer to the New Nationalism of Theodore Roosevelt and the intellectuals associated with the *New Republic* than to Woodrow Wilson's New Freedom. Given the triumph of industrialism and capitalism, he asked pointedly the year before publication of the *Jeffersonian Democracy* book, "What message has the sage of Monticello for us? What message have the statesmen and their followers whose political science is derived from Jefferson...?" Wilson's goal of the "democracy of small business," Beard answer-ed bluntly, was as "equally unreal and unattainable" as Jefferson's dream of agrarian democracy.[49]

But if big government was inevitable and beneficent, the problem remained of making such government effi-cient, responsible, and responsive to the popular will. One answer was through improved personnel—through, as he put it, training "thousands of young men and women for service in American democracy."[50] Thus, he was an enthusiastic admirer of the pioneering efforts of the New York Bureau of Municipal Research to train people in public administration through field work. In 1915, he became supervisor of instruction at the Bureau's Training School for Public Service, and three years later he became director of the Bureau.[51]

Although evangelical in his zeal to attract gifted young people into public service, Beard realized that institutional changes were also required. Influenced by Frank J. Goodnow, one of his professors while a graduate student at Columbia, he took over Goodnow's dichotomy between politics—or policy-making—on the one hand—and administration—or policy execution—on the other.[52] Convinced that the separation of powers so hallowed in American political mythology impeded effective action, Beard championed the principle of centralizing responsibility for policy implementation in the executive. Thus, he provided the intellectual rationale for the sweeping reorganization of New York state government pushed through by Al Smith during the 1920's. And in line with his and the staff's interest in "public administration as a science," Beard laid the ground work for the reorganization of the Bureau into the Institute of Public Adminstration. [53]

Beard resigned as director of the Bureau in 1920. In part, he wanted more time for his own historical research and writing. In part, he was upset over the political storm roused by the Bureau's recommendations to deal with the New York transit crisis, bored with the administrative routine, and tired of the hassles of fund-raising. There was anxiety among the Bureau's board of directors—shared by Beard himself—that his reputation for radicalism was impairing the Bureau's ability to attract funding.[54] At the same time, Beard had begun to have his doubts about the Bureau's narrow focus on the purely "technical aspects" of urban planning and policy-making.[55] He even questioned whether "a democratic government [can] conceive and carry out any large collective program other than war." Innumerable examples of the strength of vested interests in blocking reform, he lamented to the 1925 meeting of the National Conference on the Science of Politics, "seem to point to a negative answer." [56]

But such pessimism was not typical of Beard in the 1920's. Despite the waning of the reform spirit, his own hopes for the future burned ever more brightly. Publishing in collaboration with his wife his monumental *The Rise of American Civilization* in 1927, he traced the triumph of capitalism and the capitalists. Yet he was far from disheartened over what lay ahead. The 1920's were, he concluded, "the dawn, not the dusk, of the gods." The triumph of the plutocracy had been made possible by the break-up of the South-West alliance between planters and free farmers. The fight over the McNary-Haugen farm relief bill—which he strongly favored—betokened "that the old union may again be renewed under a broader social philosophy and more competent leadership." He extolled the progress made since the beginning of the century in enacting "humane and democratic legislation running in the direction of greater economic justice." He described in glowing terms the growth in "concrete services rendered to the people" by government at all levels. And he was confident that the expanded role of government—that the rise of the "Leviathan"—would increase, not reduce, "the freedom of the individual." [57]

Beard was not unmindful of the contributions made by innumerable men and women through agitation, pressure, and political action to the achievement of these gains. But what most sustained his hopes for a future of "unlimited progress" was his confidence in the inexorable forces set loose by the Industrial Revolution—the triumph of the machine and the rise of modern science. The machine age had its own inner logic: its hallmarks were cooperation, order, and control. Widening government regulation, even increasing government ownership and operation, Beard wrote in his 1928 symposium on the future of modern civilization, "will come about gradually as a necessity of the machine system." Progress was thus not simply unlimited, but certain, inevitable, even automatic. "By inherent necessity," he affirmed in a follow-up symposium for a group of engineers, the machine process "forces upon society an ever larger planned area of conduct." [58]

Yet by the time these words were published, the country had begun its slide into the depths of the Great Depression. And Beard's hopes for the future of American democracy were further threatened by totalitarian ideologies offering their own panaceas for the collapse of capitalism.

Beard was briefly attracted by Mussolini's corporatism. But his enthusiasm was shortlived.[59] He never had any illusions about Nazism. Nazi Germany, he told an audience at the New School for Social Research in April, 1934, was "government by irresponsible brute force, by unquestioning and unchallenged berserker rage." Breaking his rule against lending his name to committees, he served as honorary Chairman of the International Relief Association to assist victims of Hitler's terror. And Beard had no doubts that Hitler planned war as soon as the time was ripe.[60]

Nor did he find the extreme left any more to his way of thinking. During the 1930's he reread Marx and Engels. But his reading simply reinforced his rejection of Marxism. "The essence of Marxism," was "violence"—and thus Marxists repudiated "freedom of press, liberty of conscience, personal rights, democracy, the settlement of social conflicts by rational processes."[61] As early as 1931, he saw the Soviet Union as a land of "political and economic despotism" ruled "by tyranny and terror, with secret police, espionage, and arbitrary executions." He scornfully dismissed the American Communists as puppets and agents of the Soviet tyranny and warned his fellow liberals against collaboration with the party.[62]

At the same time, the Depression had laid bare the inadequacy, indeed, the impossibility, of laissez-faire.[63] What then was the alternative? Beard rejected nationalization of industry, even of the railroads and electric power business.[64] Instead, he called for "national planning"—the application by democratic government of what he called "engineering rationality"—to coordinate and rationalize the economy. He was hazy, even indifferent, about the detailed implementation of this national planning. And he too readily assumed that national planning would be compatible with those features of American life he cherished: its "traditions of personal liberty," its "long-continued institutions of local government," its "easy-going democracy of customs," its spirit of "enterprise," "efficiency," and "ingenuity." But he was not so much concerned with drafting a detailed blue-print for the future as with conveying a message of hope—that "America has the intelligence, the organizing capacity, the engineering skill, the material endowment, and above all, men and women...[with] faith in the mission of their country" to attain new heights "far beyond our dim, chill imaginations." [65]

Beard warned, however, that the prerequisite for fulfilling that hope was the resolution of what he saw as the larger and more fundamental crisis in thought facing Western civilization. The scientific-technological revolution had destroyed the "theological supremacy and assurance" of the past. In its place had emerged the new faith that science—the empirical method—could provide "unequivocal guidance...for human conduct and policy." In his younger days, Beard himself had subscribed to that faith. But the experience of totalitarian regimes abroad had shown that science could be employed for ill as much as for beneficent purposes. He did not question the value of the scientific method in showing the "most appropriate and promising ways and means" of realizing society's purposes. What he denied was that science could provide those goals; "the very essence of science" was "neutrality." Since an "action or thing can be desirable only with reference to some posited or assumed standard of good or beauty," he called for "a frank recognition of the fact that ethics and esthetics underlie and are essential to the operation of any great society." [66]

The Depression coupled with the totalitarian challenges shattered beyond repair his former optimistic faith in inevitable and automatic progress. Yet Beard did not abandon his belief in progress. What was new in the 1930's was his insistence that progress required "immense efforts of will and intelligence": that men must consciously and willfully act to create a future still in the making. Beard took over as his own a three-part formula derived from Machiavelli. "In human affairs," he explained, "are to be found <u>necessity</u> or things inescapable, <u>fortune</u> or the appearances of choice, and <u>virtue</u> or the capacity for choice and action." Although limited by the "necessities and possibilities" of the American situation—geography, the state of technology, the availability of resources, and the like—statesmen had the capacity, indeed, were faced with the necessity, for making choices based upon "ethical and esthetic values." [67]

This new approach was inextricably intertwined with Beard's conversion to historical relativism. The finite mind, Beard admonished in his 1933 presidential address to the American Historical Association, could not possibly comprehend all of "history as actuality." Nor did facts select or arrange themselves "automatically" in the mind of the historian. The "selection and arrangement of facts" was "an act of choice" reflecting the historian's "frame of reference"—his values and interests, his political, social, and economic beliefs, his conception of "things deemed necessary, things deemed possible, and things deemed desirable." Given the limitations of the historian's knowledge of the past—and given further an indeterminate future shapable by human will and actions—Beard denied the possibility of "a science of history" capable of subsuming under law all past, present, and future occurrences and thus making possible "the calculable prediction of the future." [68]

At times, Beard even questioned if any history could be more than "impressionistic eclecticism." [69] But he recoiled from the nihilistic implications of unlimited relativism. Driven by a deep psychological need to provide a rationale for his life-long commitment to the idea of history as a guide to the future, he demanded that the historian make a judgment about the "nature or direction" of history as a whole. And he insisted that there were only three possible alternatives: history as flux or chaos, history as a process of cyclical recurrence, or history as progressive development "on an upward gradient toward a more ideal order." He saw no objective way of choosing among these alternatives; an appeal to the facts would be inconclusive. The historian must make "an act of faith." Beard's own "act of faith" was that history—at least in the United States—was moving forward to "a collectivist democracy."[70]

After his dismay over the paralysis afflicting the last days of the Hoover administration,[71] Beard hailed the New Deal as "The Future Comes." He had praise for nearly every achievement of the First Hundred Days. But he waxed most enthusiastic about the National Industrial Recovery Act for recognizing the historical trend toward consolidation and cooperation in industry, for accelerating that process, and for providing for business "self-regulation" under government "supervision" and "control." "Implicit" in the "Recovery Program," he wrote enthusiastically, was "a changed conception of economy and life": an abandonment of the "speculative" ideal "of getting rich as quickly as possible" in favor of "reasonable security for all." The New Deal was thus new, even revolutionary—"a break with the historic past and the coming of a future collectivist in character."[72]

As time passed, however, Beard grew more and more disturbed at the failure of the New Deal to fulfill his hopes. At the beginning of 1935, he was lamenting that the New Deal had failed to bring about economic recovery, that the Roosevelt administration lacked any effective policy to bring about an "equitable distribution of wealth," and that business—rather than the "little fellow"—had benefited most from the existing New Deal programs. "Not a single instrumentality of economic power," he complained, "has been wrested" from the "party of wealth and talents." He even predicted that at the end of the Depression—"if it ever ends"—the concentration of wealth would have reached "a new high point in the evolution of American economy." Worse still was that Roosevelt was failing to provide effective leadership to meet the nation's problems. The chief executive, he bluntly charged, appeared "at the end of his resources so far as domestic policy is concerned."[73]

Not even the remarkable burst of legislation of the

Second Hundred Days assuaged his anxieties. Millions remained unemployed. The national debt was growing at an alarming rate. But what most distressed him was the administration's retreat from national planning, a retreat symbolized by the rising influence of the neo-Brandeisians with their "deep-seated belief in 'the curse of bigness.' " Assailing "the cult of littleness and federal impotence," Beard called for "big government at Washington" to provide the "coordination, planning and supervision" required to make the "giant national economy interdependent in all its parts," function at its full potential. [74]

Beard was a frequent visitor to Washington during these years, keeping his eyes on events, advising government officials and political leaders, and serving as a member of the consumers' advisory board of the National Recovery Administration. [75] Back home in Connecticut, he championed the AAA marketing agreements among his fellow dairymen, and when the state's milk producers threatened a strike in protest against low prices, he was instrumental in working out a settlement. [76] He was appalled and indignant over the scandals involving the nation's financial leaders filling the newspapers. "Oh! those *respectable* ones," he exclaimed to Matthew Josephson, or so Josephson recalled," — oh! their *temples* of respectability — how I detest them, how I would love to pull them all down!" And as the owner of defaulted bonds of the Missouri Pacific Railroad, he organized an Independent Bondholders Committee to resist the financial manipulations of the Morgan-Van Sweringen interests. [77]

Beard's major contribution to the New Deal — and the contribution most appreciated by the Roosevelt administration [78] — was his defense of the constitutionality of the New Deal measures. He had no doubt that the decisions of the Supreme Court restricting "the powers of government within the narrowest possible limits" were "in flat contradiction to the intentions of the framers." What more sweeping grants of power, he asked, could be imagined than the "necessary and proper" and "general welfare" clauses? Even Jefferson—the hero of the Liberty League—"took a broad view of the Constitution in practice" as "adequate to all the grand national policies which the exigencies of the hour seemed to demand." [79]

At the same time, Beard had no sympathy with proposals to strip the Supreme Court of its power to pass on acts of Congress. Though admitting that the Court "has not been very hot in its defense of personal liberties and rights," he questioned what Congress would do—given the recurring vigilantism that swept the country—if "turned loose without bridle or rider." He was dubious about suggested constitutional amendments to give Congress added authority. The political obstacles to any amendment were formidable, perhaps insuperable, and hostile judges could nullify even the broadest grant of powers. Beard's own solution was simply to rely upon "Father Time"—the inexorable march of events and ideas. But he did suggest, on the eve of the 1936 elections, as a possible way of speeding up "Father Time" President Grant's example in the legal tender cases: the appointment of new justices "of the right kind." [80]

Despite the shortcomings of the New Deal, Beard continued to rest his hopes for the future on F.D.R. "Your acceptance address," he and his wife wired Roosevelt in June, 1936, marks "in spirit and thought the opening of a new epoch in American public life." "As a life-long student of American history," he wrote F.D.R.'s secretary after Roosevelt's second inaugural address, "I am convinced that no President, not even Washington and Jefferson, ever wrote state papers that went wider and deeper into fundamentals." He publicly expressed his optimism that the chief executive would take advantage of his overwhelming mandate in the 1936 election to push forward with "some new effort" to "organize national industries with a view to speeding up production, absorbing more of the unemployed, and raising labor standards." [81] When Roosevelt in February sent Congress his proposal to increase the number of Supreme Court

justices, Beard took to the air waves to defend the plan as
a justified and "constitutional" way of bringing "the Court
back within the Constitution." And after the Court made
its famous "switch in time," he congratulated the President
for having "won the battle...to preserve the balance of
powers in government as distinguished from judicial
supremacy." [82]

But when he came to sum up the New Deal years on the
eve of the 1940 elections, Beard sadly concluded that
though Roosevelt may have won that battle, the larger war
had been lost. Though still finding much to praise in the
New Deal, he blasted Roosevelt's failure to follow through
with a "cooperative, concerted plan for industrial order
and progress," his failure to put the nation's productive
capacity fully to work, and his failure to solve "the major
problem of concentration in private ownership of the
greater part of the country's resources and productive
plant, with its consequent private control over production
and prices." With national planning abandoned, and with
"direct government ownership of industrial properties
along socialistic lines" not even contemplated, the
administration had come to rely upon a continuing high
level of government spending to keep the economy
"running at even a moderate tempo." Such government
spending, Beard warned, could supply no more than a
temporary and artificial fillip to the economy, while the
growing national debt portended a new and graver
"explosion." [83]

Beard's disillusionment with the New Deal fueled his
anxieties about Roosevelt's foreign policies. From the start,
he had worried lest F.D.R. attempt to solve the Depression
by pushing to expand markets abroad for this country's
surpluses. [84] And he watched with dismay the growing
ascendancy of "the sentimental internationalists" — led by
Secretary of State Cordell Hull — over the economic
nationalists such as George N. Peek. His sympathies in the
struggle over administration trade policies lay with
Peek — "the realist among the administration men engaged

on the foreign trade side. The others are more or less boggled up with Manchesterism and imperialistic delusions."[85] Even during the 1920's Beard had warned that the pursuit of "trade and profits" in the Far East would lead to a clash with Japan.[86] The world-wide scramble for markets spurred by the Depression made the danger of "a futile and idiotic war in the Far Pacific" loom the more ominously in his mind.[87]

The worsening tensions in Europe exacerbated his anxieties. As the failure of the New Deal to restore prosperity became more and more apparent, Beard grew more and more suspicious that Roosevelt, having exhausted his bag of tricks on the domestic front, was looking to divert the American people by foreign adventures. The administration's reliance upon government spending to keep the economy afloat reinforced that tendency. The rationale of national defense silenced the "constant and savage nagging" that had threatened the New Deal's spending program. Worse, Roosevelt—like Wilson before him—had become infected with "world lecturing and interventionism" and had become infatuated with the delusion that he was "commissioned to set the world aright."[88] Long before Pearl Harbor, Beard was convinced that F.D.R. was determined to bring this country into the struggle against Hitler—and that if he could not do so directly, then he would do so by the "roundabout way" of provoking a war with Japan.[89]

Beard's revulsion against foreign entanglements reinforced his belief that America was a distinctive and unique civilization, a land without the feudal past, class bitterness, and time-encrusted hatreds and feuds of the Old World, a land with its own special genius and destiny.[90] In *The American Spirit*—which was published in 1942 as the final volume of "The Rise of American Civilization" series—Beard and his wife attempted to set forth this country's "unique features in origins, substance, and development." The book interpreted American history in Manichaean terms as a struggle between the forces of light and the representatives of darkness: the champions of a democratic collectivism versus the selfish and self-interested defenders of an outmoded individualism and status quo. The complex of beliefs and values that constituted the American "idea of civilization" included "respect for life, for human worth, for the utmost liberty..., for equality of rights and opportunities, for the dignity and utility of labor, for the rule of universal participation in the work and benefits of society." But its most important tenet was its optimistic faith in the ability of "human intelligence" to shape the future: the American people's commitment to the "endless" struggle "for individual and social perfection—for the good, the true, the beautiful— against ignorance, disease, the harshness of physical nature, the forces of barbarism in individuals and in society." [91]

The corollary of Beard's own commitment to these beliefs and values was his revitalized appreciation of the virtues of the American system of government. He extolled the United States Constitution—with its balance between majority rule and "fundamental rights" that government, even majorities, could not transgress—as "in eternal contradiction to the principle of authoritarian, totalitarian, dictatorial government." Whereas he had formerly assailed the separation of powers as a barrier to reform, he now praised the system of checks and balances as preventing "the accumulation of despotic power in any hands, even in the hands of the people." Abandoned was his economic interpretation of the Founding Fathers. In their *A Basic History of the United States*, he and his wife stressed the framers' "national vision...rising above purely personal interests," portrayed their handiwork as simultaneously preserving the Union from collapse while averting a threatened "military dictatorship," and hailed their foresight in making "the instrument flexible for adaption to changes in the needs, ideas, and interests of the American people." [92]

But his celebration of the past was accompanied by

deep pessimism about the present and the future. Although the war had converted many former isolationists to collective security, Beard looked with suspicion and hostility upon this country's membership in the United Nations as a threat to American independence and sovereignty.[93] He feared that the aggrandizement of executive power under the New Deal had done grave, perhaps irreparable, damage to American institutions.[94] He was convinced that F.D.R. had deceived and misled the American people by plotting war while talking peace—and he was further convinced that, in so doing, F.D.R. had brought the republic to the verge of Caesarism.[95] The war had diverted and dissipated reform, left the country saddled with a "stupendous" national debt and "grinding taxes," and had accelerated the trend to an ever more powerful—and now not so benevolent—Leviathan. And the emergence of "a gigantic military and naval establishment" portended a "menace to civilian life and civilian government." [96]

Beard's bitterness over American involvement in World War II was heightened by his all-too-painful awareness that the defeat of Hitler had not assured this country's safety and security. He was haunted by the specter of the atomic bomb with its threat of world destruction. And he saw Russia—a "totalitarian regime no less despotic and ruthless" than Nazi Germany and "equally inimical to the democracy, liberties, and institutions of the United States"—emerge from the conflict the "dominant power" astride Europe and Asia.[97] Beard had no sympathy with pro-Soviet apologists in this country.[98] But he instinctively recoiled from the Truman administration's containment policies. He even accused the administration of plotting war with Russia—of looking for another "Pearl Harbor." "The Democrats," he complained angrily early in 1948, "are playing the old game of crisis and trying to wring one more victory out of the bloody shirt! Having brought the country to the verge of disaster, they want to complete the job." [99]

Yet Beard never succumbed to despair. He continued to hope that the American people might yet learn from experience and pull back from the precipice—and that his own exposure of the "discrepancies between official representations and official realities" in Roosevelt's foreign policies would contribute to this awakening.[100] He had suffered a serious illness in 1945.[101]   And his work—"day and night" [102] —on the two Roosevelt foreign policy books further undermined his formerly robust constitution.   But immediately after publication of *Roosevelt and the Coming of the War*, he plunged into work upon a follow-up study of wartime diplomacy. "I have written two books about this war," he vowed to Raymond Moley. "I will write more, if I live." He died September 1, 1948, "a victim," Moley eulogized, "of hard work induced by a passionate drive to tell the truth as he saw it...his frail body literally charred and killed by the drive of his burning mind." [103]

What was Beard's legacy? Even his sharpest critics admit that Beard was the most influential—indeed, the most seminal—figure in twentieth-century American historical thought. But perhaps more importantly, the issues to which he addressed himself still face the American people. The relationship between impersonal forces and personal responsibility, between ideas and interests, between the individual and society; the role of government in the economy, the proper balance between freedom and authority, the place of the United States in the world; how to make government efficient yet responsible and responsive, how to preserve freedom of opinion and expression in a mass society, and how to fulfill the American dream of equality and justice for all without destroying individual liberty and initiative—all these problems remain with us to this day and will probably continue to agitate our minds as long as the United States survives. In dealing with these problems, Beard brought a high intelligence, a hatred for sham and hypocrisy, and a passionate moral sense. Though we may not agree with all his answers, his example should stand as an inspiration to us—and to generations not yet born.

Notes

1. *New York Times,* May 26, 1940; Raymond Moley, 27 *Masters of Politics: In a Personal Perspective* (New York, 1949), p. 15; Matthew Josephson, "Charles A. Beard: A Memoir," *Virginia Quarterly Review* 25 (1949): 589.
2. Beard to Gardner L. Harding, December 20 [1934], George N. Peek Papers, Western Historical Manuscript Collection, University of Missouri Library; *New York Times,* April 16, 1939; Beard to Oswald Garrison Villard, [c. 1948], Villard Papers, Houghton Library, Harvard University.
3. James T. Shotwell Memoir, p. 62, Columbia Oral History Collection; Moley, 27 *Masters of Politics,* p. 15.
4. Beard, "Political Science," in Wilson Gee, ed., *Research in the Social Sciences: Its Fundamental Methods and Objectives* (New York, 1929), p. 287.
5. Howard K. Beale, ed., *Charles A. Beard: A Reappraisal* (Lexington, Ky., 1954), p. 7.
6. Carl L. Becker, review of Beard's *Cross Currents in Europe To-Day, Nation,* November 22, 1922, p. 553; Irwin Edman, *Philosopher's Holiday* (New York, 1938), p. 131; Mary Beard to Rosika Schwimmer, July 25, 1936, Schwimmer-Lloyd Collection, New York Public Library.
7. Beale, *Beard,* p. 156.
8. *New York Times,* January 23, February 13, 1938.
9. Beard to Curtice N. Hitchcock, June 11, 1927, Macmillan Company Records, New York Public Library; Mary Beard to Blanche Knoph, February 25, 1939, Knoph Papers (in possession of Mr. Alfred A. Knoph), July 17, 1974.
10. *New York Times,* July 18, November 12, 1915; January 31, 1916.
11. Beard, "That Promise of American Life," *New Republic,* February 6, 1935, pp. 351-52.
12. Beard, "The World As I Want It," *Forum and Century,* June 1934, pp. 332-34.
13. Shotwell Memoir, p. 63.
14. Beard to Albert J. Beveridge, October 24 [1917], Beveridge Papers, Library of Congress.
15. Beard, "Political Science," pp. 289-90.
16. Beard to Arthur M. Schlesinger, July 23 [1917], April 7, 1946, Schlesinger Papers, Harvard University Archives.
17. Beard to R. Walton Moore, January 10, 1936, OF 2039, Franklin D. Roosevelt Papers, Roosevelt Library; Beard to George Novack, September 26 [1936], in Harold Kirker and Burleigh Taylor Wilkins, "Beard, Becker and the Trotsky Inquiry," *American Quarterly* 13 (1961): 518.
18. Beard and Birl E. Schultz, *Documents on the State-wide Initiative, Referendum and Recall* (New York, 1912), pp. 1-69.
19. See, for example, *New York Times,* October 12, 1919.

20.   Beard and Mary R. Beard, *The American Spirit: A Study of the Idea of Civilization in the United States* (1942; paperback ed., New York, 1962), p. 7.

21.   Newspaper clippings, April-May 1916, and typewritten "Statement of Facts in the Matter of the Committee of Education of the Board of Trustees of Columbia University and Professor Charles A. Beard" [1916], Beard File (microfilm), DePauw University Archives.

22.   Shotwell Memoir, p. 68; Beard, "The Supreme Issue," *New Republic*, January 18, 1919, p. 343; Beard, "On the Advantages of Censorship and Espionage," *ibid.*, August 24, 1921, pp. 350-51; Beard, "Count Karolyi and America," *Nation*, April 1, 1925, pp. 347-48; *New York Times*, March 8, 1925, April 3, 1940; Josephson, "Beard: Memoir," 592.

23.   Beard, "Time, Technology, and the Creative Spirit in Political Science," *American Political Science Review* 21 (1927): 11.

24.   Beale, *Beard*, pp. 215, 241-42; Alvin Johnson, *Pioneer's Progress* (1952; paperback ed., Lincoln, Neb., 1960), pp. 167, 273, 276, 278; Beard, "The Dislocated Soldier of Industry," in Morse A. Cartwright, ed., *Unemployment and Adult Education: A Symposium*...(New York, 1931), pp. 9-12; Guy Stanton Ford Memoir, 4: 630-31, 633-37, 639, Columbia Oral History Collection; Educational Policies Commission, National Education Association, *The Unique Function of Education in American Democracy* (Washington, D.C., 1937), "Acknowledgement"; C.A. Bowers, *The Progressive Educator and the Depression: The Radical Years* (New York, 1969, pp. 114, 128, 167; *New York Times,* May 21, 1936; Beard to Franklin D. Roosevelt, August 31, 1936, PPF 3847, Roosevelt Papers.

25.   Beard, *A Charter for the Social Sciences in the Schools* (Report of the Commission on the Social Studies, Part I) (New York, 1932), p. 116; Beard, "Conditions Favorable to Creative Work in Political Science," in *Report of the Committee on Policy of the American Political Science Association* [Supplement to *American Political Science Review* 24, no. 1 (February 1930)], pp. 28-29.

26.   American Historical Association, Commission on the Social Studies, *Conclusions and Recommendations of the Commission* (New York, 1934), p. 16. On Beard as the primary author of this report, see Ford Memoir, 4: 633-37, 639. Harry D. Gideonse, "Nationalist Collectivism and Charles A. Beard," *Journal of Political Economy* 43 (1935): 778-81, is a critical appraisal.

27.   *New York Times*, October 22, 1939; April 9, 1943.

28.   Richard Hofstadter and Walter P. Metzger, *The Development of Academic Freedom in the United States* (New York, 1955), pp. 498-502; Carol S. Gruber, "Mars and Minerva: World War I and the American Academic Man" (Ph.D. diss., Columbia University, 1968), pp. 227-49; newspaper clippings, October 1917, DePauw Beard file; "A Statement by Charles A. Beard," *New Republic*, December 29, 1917, pp. 249-50.

29. Robert W. Iversen, *The Communists and the Schools* (New York, 1959), pp. 166-67.

30. Beard, "Mine Eyes May Behold," *New Republic*, January 19, 1938, p. 306; Gruber, "Mars and Minerva," pp. 225-27.

31. *New York Times*, February 25, 1935; *New Republic*, March 11, 1936, p. 122; Beard to Roosevelt, August 31, 1936, PPF 3847, Roosevelt Papers.

32. On Beard and the climate of opinion, see: Morton G. White, *American Social Thought: The Revolt against Formalism* (New York, 1949), pp. 7-8, 11-15, 27-58, 107-27, 220-44; Eric Goldman, "The Origins of Beard's *Economic Interpretation of the Constitution*," *Journal of the History of Ideas* 13 (1952): 234-49; Richard Hofstadter, *The Progressive Historians: Turner, Beard, Parrington* (New York, 1968), pp. 181-203.

33. Beard to George P. Brett, September 3, 1907, Macmillan Company Records; Herbert Pell Memoir, 1:62, Columbia Oral History Collection.

34. Beard, *Politics* (New York, 1908), pp. 20, 26, 33; Beard, *An Economic Interpretation of the Constitution of the United States* (1935 ed.; paperback ed., New York, 1965), pp. 15-16.

35. James Harvey Robinson and Beard, *The Development of Modern Europe: An Introduction to the Study of Current History*, 2 vols. (Boston, New York, Chicago, and London, 1907-08), 1:iii.

36. Beard, review of James Ford Rhodes, *History of the United States 1877-1896*, *New Republic*, December 17, 1919, p. 83.

37. Beard, *The Industrial Revolution* (1901; reprint ed., New York, 1969), pp. 53, 86.

38. Beard, *American City Government: A Survey of Newer Tendencies* (New York, 1912), p. 386.

39. Beard, *Contemporary American History 1877-1913* (New York, 1914), pp. 307-08.

40. Beard to Schlesinger, June 30, 1915, Schlesinger Papers; Beard to Beveridge, January 15, 1919, Beveridge Papers.

41. Beard, *The Supreme Court and the Constitution*, with an Introduction and Bibliography by Alan F. Westin (Englewood Cliffs, N.J., 1962), pp. 25, 69.

42. *Ibid.*, pp. 84, 94.

43. R. Gordon Hoxie, *et al.*, *A History of the Faculty of Political Science Columbia University* (New York, 1955), p. 265; Beard to Schlesinger, May 14, July 23 [1917], Schlesinger Papers.

44. Beard, *An Economic Interpretation*, pp. xix, vi.

45. *Marion Star*, May 3, 1913, clipping, DePauw Beard File.

46. Herbert Croly, *Progressive Democracy* (New York, 1914), pp. 48-50, 230-31.

47. *New York Times*, January 18, 1915.

48. Beard, *Economic Origins of Jeffersonian Democracy* (1915; paperback ed., New York, 1965), pp. 464, 446.

49. Beard, "Jefferson and the New Freedom," *New Republic*, November 14, 1914, pp. 18-19. On his ties with the *New Republic*

group, see Charles Forcey, *The Crossroads of Liberalism: Croly, Weyl, Lippmann, and the Progressive Era* (New York, 1961), p. 208; for his later praise of the 1912 Progressive Party platform, see Beard, "Looking Backward," *New Republic*, November 8, 1939, pp. 74, 76, 78.

50.   Beard to Schlesinger, March 24, 1917, Schlesinger Papers.

51.   Jane S. Dahlberg, *The New York Bureau of Municipal Research: Pioneer in Government Administration* (New York, 1966), pp. 25-26, 130-33; William Harvey Allen Memoir, 2: 210, Columbia Oral History Collection; *New York Times*, February 9, 1915, March 7, 1918.

52.   Bernard C. Borning, *The Political and Social Thought of Charles A. Beard* (Seattle, 1962), pp. 20, 81-82.

53.   Dahlberg, *New York Bureau*, pp. 93-112, 190-98; Beale, *Beard*, pp. 53-55; David M. Ellis, et al., *A History of New York State* (Ithaca, N.Y., 1967), pp. 390, 400-02; Luther Gulick to author, July 17, 1974.

54.   R. Fulton Cutting to Henry S. Pritchett, July 9, 1920, File #389 (Bureau of Municipal Research), Carnegie Foundation for the Advancement of Teaching; Gulick to author, July 17, 1974; interview with Gulick, June 16, 1974.

55.   On the Bureau's philosophy, see Dahlberg, *New York Bureau*, pp. 39-43; for Beard's criticism, see "Some Aspects of Regional Planning," *American Political Science Review* 20 (1926): 276.

56.   *New York Times*, September 8, 1925.

57.   Beard and Mary R. Beard, *The Rise of American Civilization*, 2 vols. (New York, 1927), 2:800; *New York Times*, August 3, 1927; Beard, "Recent Gains in Government," *World Tomorrow*, November 1927, pp. 438-41; Beard, ed., *Whither Mankind: A Panorama of Modern Civilization* (New York, London, and Toronto, 1928), p. 407.

58.   Beard and Beard, *Rise of American Civilization*, 2:800; Beard, *Whither Mankind*, pp. 404-06; Beard, ed., *Toward Civilization* (London, New York, and Toronto, 1930), p. 299.

59.   John P. Diggins, *Mussolini and Fascism: The View from America* (Princeton, 1972), pp. 226-27; Beard, review of Herbert W. Schneider, *The Making of the Fascist State*, *New Republic*, January 23, 1929, pp. 277-78; Beard, "A 'Five-Year Plan' for America," *Forum*, July 1931, p. 3.

60.   Beard, "Hitlerism and Our Liberties" [speech], April 10, 1934, DePauw Beard File; *New York Times*, July 20, 1936; Beard, "Education under the Nazis," *Foreign Affairs* 14 (1935-36): 452.

61.   Beard with the collaboration of G.H.E. Smith, *The Open Door at Home: A Trial Philosophy of National Interest* (New York, 1934), p. 110; Beard and Beard, *American Spirit*, p. 461.

62.   Beard, "Five-Year Plan," 3-4; Matthew Josephson, *Infidel in the Temple: A Memoir of the Nineteen-Thirties* (New York, 1967), p. 71.

63. Beard, "The Myth of Rugged American Individualism," *Harper's Magazine*, December 1931, p. 22.

64. *New York Times.* March 12, 1931.

65. Beard, "Five-Year Plan," pp. 1-11.

66. Beard, *Open Door*, pp. 4, 6, 16, 30, 139.

67. Beard, "Introduction," J.B. Bury, *The Idea of Progress: An Inquiry into Its Origins and Growth* (1932; reprint ed., New York, 1955), p. xl.; Beard, *Open Door*, p. 34. Beard's rejection of determinism is explored in detail in David W. Marcell, *Progress and Pragmatism: James, Dewey, Beard, and the American Idea of Progress* (Westport, Conn., and London, 1974), esp. pp. 292-309, 314-21.

68. Beard, "Written History as an Act of Faith," *American Historical Review* 39 (1933-34): 220-21, 227, 224. The following analyze the sources and development of Beard's relativism: Whitaker T. Deininger, "The Skepticism and Historical Faith of Charles A. Beard," *Journal of the History of Ideas* 15 (1954): 573-88; Lloyd R. Sorenson, "Charles A. Beard and German Historiographical Thought," *Mississippi Valley Historical Review* 42 (1955-56): 274-87; Cushing Stout, *The Pragmatic Revolt in American History: Carl Becker and Charles Beard* (New Haven, 1958), pp. 50-61; Gerald D. Nash, "Self-Education in Historiography: The Case of Charles A. Beard," *Pacific Northwest Quarterly* 52 (1961): 108-15; and Hugh I. Rodgers, "Charles A. Beard, the 'New Physics,' and Historical Relativity," *Historian* 30 (1967-68): 545-60.

69. Beard to Schlesinger, August 3 [1933], Schlesinger Papers.

70. Beard, "Written History," pp. 225-29.

71. Beard, "Congress under Fire," *Yale Review*, n.s. 22 (1932-33): 41.

72. Beard and George H.E. Smith, *The Future Comes: A Study of the New Deal* (New York, 1933), pp. 46, 162-64.

73. *New York Times*, March 10, 1935; Beard, "National Politics and War," *Scribner's Magazine*, February 1935, pp. 69-70; Beard, "The President Loses Prestige," *Current History*, April 1935, p. 65.

74. Beard, "The New Deal's Rough Road," *Current History*, September 1935, pp. 625-26; Beard, "America Must Stay Big," *Today*, September 14, 1935, pp. 4, 21.

75. *New York Times*, September 17, 1933.

76. Milburn Lincoln Wilson Memoir, 11: 2115-16, Columbia Oral History Collection; materials *re* threatened milk strike (August 1933), DePauw Beard File.

77. Josephson, *Infidel in the Temple*, pp. 170, 341-43; *New York Times*, March 21, April 30, 1935; note *re* Louis B. Wehle letter, May 2, 1935, OF 2039; *Supplemental Statement submitted by Charles A. Beard on behalf of Independent Bondholders Committee to Senate Committee on Interstate Commerce*, [May 2, 1935], and memorandum, Roosevelt to Jesse Jones, August 14, 1935, OF 31, Roosevelt Papers; T.R.B., "Funny Business in the ICC," *New Republic*, October 20, 1937, pp. 293-95.

78. Leo R. Sack to Roosevelt, January 2, 1936; Sack to Marvin H. McIntyre, January 2, 1936; Roosevelt to Sack, January 16, 1936, PPF 1664; Roosevelt to Beard, March 19, 1936, OF 2039, Roosevelt Papers.

79. Beard, "Little Alice Looks at the Constitution," *New Republic,* July 22, 1936, p. 317; Beard, "What About the Constitution?", *Nation,* April 1, 1936, p. 406; Beard, "Jefferson in America Now," *Yale Review,* n.s. 25 (1935-36): 252.

80. Beard, "What About the Constitution?", pp. 405-06; Beard to Nicholas Kelley, August 8, [1936], Mary Dewson Papers, Franklin D. Roosevelt Library; Beard, "Rendezvous with the Supreme Court," *New Republic,* September 2, 1936, pp. 92-94.

81. Beard and Mary R. Beard to Roosevelt, June 28, 1936 (telegram), PPF 200-B (box 69); Beard to Stephen Early, January 30, 1937, PPF 98, Roosevelt Papers; Beard, " 'Going Ahead' with Roosevelt," *Events,* January 1937, pp. 9-10.

82. "Text of Address of Dr. Charles Beard, over the National Broadcasting Company, March 29, 1937"; Beard to Roosevelt, May 29, 1937, PPF 3847, Roosevelt Papers; *New York Times,* December 28, 1937.

83. Beard and George H.E. Smith, *The Old Deal and the New* (New York, 1940), pp. 132, 172, 159, 278, 282.

84. Beard, with the collaboration of G.H.E. Smith, *The Idea of National Interest: An Analytical Study in American Foreign Policy* (New York, 1934), pp. 546-48, 552; Beard, *Open Door,* pp. 316-17.

85. Beard to Harding, December 20 [1934], Peek Papers. For the conflict over the administration's trade policies, see Gilbert C. Fite, *George N. Peek and the Fight for Farm Parity* (Norman, Okla., 1954), pp. 267-85; for Beard's support of Peek's position, Beard to George N. Peek, May 8, November 15 [1935], August 29, 1935, Peek Papers.

86. Beard, "War with Japan: What Shall We Get Out of It?", *Nation,* March 25, 1925, pp. 311-13.

87. Beard to Raymond Moley, May 18 [1935], PPF 743, Roosevelt Papers.

88. Beard, "National Politics and War," p. 70; Beard, "Peace Loads the Guns," *Today,* June 29, 1935, pp. 4, 23; Beard, *Giddy Minds and Foreign Quarrels: An Estimate of American Foreign Policy* (New York, 1939), pp. 28-57; Beard and Smith, *Old Deal and New,* pp. 168-71.

89. Beard to H.L. Mencken, [May 1939], Mencken Papers, New York Public Library; Beard to Harry Elmer Barnes, May 30 [1940], Barnes Papers, Archive of Contemporary History, University of Wyoming Library; Beard, "Crisis in the Pacific, I—War with Japan?", *Events,* November 1940, pp. 321-23; Beard to Villard, April 15, 1947, Villard Papers.

90. *New York Times,* October 22, 1939.

91. Beard and Beard, *American Spirit,* pp. 580-81. For a perceptive analysis of this work, see Robert A. Skotheim, *American Intellectual Histories and Historians* (Princeton, 1966), pp. 105-09.

92. Beard, *The Republic: Conversations on Fundamentals* (New York, 1943), p. 16; Beard and Mary R. Beard, *A Basic History of the United States* (Philadelphia, 1944), pp. 131, 125, 121, 133.

93. Beard, *Republic*, pp. 307-08, 315-16, 325-30; Mary Beard to Edith Wynner, May 9, 29, 1944, Wynner Papers, Schwimmer-Lloyd Collection; Beard to Villard, September 8 [1945], Villard Papers; Beard to Lindsay Rogers, March 14, 1945, [December 12, 1947], January 14, 1947 [1948], Rogers Papers, Columbia University Library.

94. Beard and Smith, *Old Deal and New*, pp. 279-81.

95. Beard, *President Roosevelt and the Coming of the War, 1941: A Study in Appearances and Realities* (New Haven, 1948), p. 598.

96. *Ibid.*, pp. 578-79; Beard, *The Economic Basis of Politics*, 3rd ed. (New York, 1945), pp. 95-99, 101-03; *New York Times*, April 4, 1948.

97. Beale, *Beard*, pp. 252, 235; Beard to Ferdinand Eberstadt, August 25, 1945, with attached memorandum "Propositions for Consideration," August 27, 1945, in Calvin L. Christman, "Charles A. Beard, Ferdinand Eberstadt, and America's Postwar Security," *Mid-America* 54 (1972): 191; Beard, *Roosevelt and the Coming of the War*, p. 577.

98. Beard to Barnes, [marked c. 1944 but probably c. November 1945], Barnes Papers; Beard to Herbert Hoover, November 17, 1945, Post-Presidential Individual, box 274, Hoover Papers, Hoover Presidential Library; Beard to Villard, November 8, 1946, April 13 [1948], Villard Papers.

99. Beard to Barnes, February 18, 1946, May 5 [1947], December 10, 1947, January 6, 1948, Barnes Papers; Beard to Villard, March 9, July 1, September 8, 1947, January 17, February 10, 1948, Villard Papers; Beard to James Putnam, January 6, 1948, Macmillan Company Records; Beard, *Roosevelt and the Coming of the War*, p. 580.

100. Beard, *Roosevelt and the Coming of the War*, p. 573; Beard to Villard, April 13 [1948], Villard Papers.

101. Beard to Rogers, March 14, 1945, Rogers Papers.

102. Beard to Hoover, December 13, 1945, Post-Presidential Individual, box 274, Hoover Papers.

103. Beard to Barnes, May 23 [1948], June 3, 1948, Barnes Papers; Moley, *27 Masters of Politics*, p. 16.

Henry Steele Commager

Mr. Commager received his education including the Ph.D. degree at the University of Chicago. Before going to Amherst in 1956, where he is currently the John Woodruff Simpson Lecturer, Mr. Commager was a member of the faculty at New York University and Columbia University, and had served as Pitt Professor of American History at Cambridge University, Harmsworth Professor of American History at Oxford University, Gottesman Professor at Uppsala University, Watson Lecturer at London University and Visiting Professor of American History at the University of Copenhagen.

Mr. Commager served on the War Department's Committee on the History of the War during and after World War II. He is a member of the American Academy of Arts and Letters and was awarded their Gold Medal for History in 1972, a medal which had been awarded Charles A. Beard in 1939. In addition to 35 honorary degrees from colleges and universities here and abroad, Mr. Commager is a member of numerous professional organizations, and an Honorary Fellow of Peterhouse, Cambridge.

Mr. Commager is the author of many books, the most recent being *Britain Through American Eyes* (1974) and *Jefferson, Nationalism and the Enlightenment* (1975), and is a frequent contributor to journals. Mr. Commager enjoyed a special relationship with Charles A. Beard, being his successor at Columbia University and teaching the constitutional history course that Beard taught.

Charles A. Beard: A Study in Paradox

Henry Steele Commager

James Farrell recalled that when he interviewed Beard
back in 1939, Beard said to him, as he left, "I wish you
would mention the fact that the faculty of Old DePauw did
more for me than I could ever tell."

Beard was indeed a son of DePauw, but that is, in a
sense, a symbol. He was—like Turner and Parrington, like
Veblen and Jane Addams—a child of the Middle Border, a
beneficiary of and contributor to the intellectual ferment
which seethed in Chicago and Madison and in other
Middle Border cities. He had listened to Bryan give his
Cross of Gold speech and as a student he had visited Hull
House and come to know Jane Addams, to whose
philosophy he was, like John Dewey, deeply indebted. But
no more than Dewey or Veblen can Beard be associated
with one climate. He was part of Populism, to be sure,
even more he was part of that progressivism which we
associate with the urban East. He was indebted to English
radicalism—had he not after all helped found Ruskin
College—and the very choice of the name is illuminating.
He had come under the influence of labor radicals like Keir
Hardie and of the Fabians. He had lectured at workingmen's institutes and he had written a book on the Industrial Revolution.

All, as it turned out, was grist to his mill, for he absorbed social and political expertise and experience like a sponge. No less important than practical experience—and he was always to indulge himself in this—no other American historian, not even Bancroft, was less of a closet philosopher than Charles Beard—was Beard's exposure to that profound intellectual revolution which we associate with the impact of Darwinian evolution. For Beard was part of—and eventually spokesman for—that new pragmatic philosophy which swept over the country at the turn of the century, and which revolutionized not only science but philosophy, law, history, politics, even the arts. What moulded his mind was not so much the Middle Border, though the influence was always there, as the city, industry, labor unions, the factory system, the new immigration, the rise of the welfare state. What influenced him was Riis's *How the Other Half Lives* and William James's *Psychology* and Lester Ward's *Psychic Factors in Civilization*, and Thorstein Veblen's *Theory of the Leisure Class* and *Theory of Business Enterprise*, and E. A. Ross's *Sin and Society*; the new jurisprudence of Justice Holmes and Roscoe Pound and Ernest Freund of the University of Chicago, and the new sociology of Ward and Patten and Giddings, and the new economics of Ely and Commons and his Columbia colleague E.A. Seligman, the new political radicalism of an Altgeld, a Pingree, a Tom Johnson and a Henry George.

With John Dewey, Beard carried much of this to Columbia and—doubtless learned much of it at Columbia which—in those far-off days—had some claim to be the liveliest intellectual center in the country and with Wisconsin (and notwithstanding President Butler) the most radical. What a galaxy of scholars Beard could associate with: Shotwell and Hayes among the historians, and James Harvey Robinson with whom he wrote that famous *Development of Modern Europe*; Seligman and Clark and Wesley Mitchell in economics; Giddings in sociology and Goodnow in politics and Boas in anthropology, and Harlan Stone and Reed Powell in the law school and, towering over them all, the benign figure of John Dewey.

Young Beard had begun life as a journalist—that was even before he turned to DePauw—and shifted next to the fascinating task of labor agitator and organizer in a foreign country. It was not to be expected that he would confine himself to the academy, and indeed Beard's formal academic career was comparatively brief, for he chose to resign, dramatically, from Columbia University in 1917, and on an issue which made him a hero of the academy for the rest of his life. He was a freelance journalist (a wonderfully appropriate term for he did indeed offer his lance free to all the good causes); he was the most successful of all textbook writers of modern history; he directed New York's Training School for Public Service; he was an advisor to the governments of Japan and Yugoslavia; he was an indefatigable scholar; he was president of both the American Historical Association and the American Political Science Association; he was a farmer—far more than a gentleman farmer, too. Indeed, what was he not! Not since Bancroft had there been anyone who combined scholarly and public contributions and enterprise so effectively—or so voluminously—as Mr. Beard.

How refreshing it all was to a hard-headed and practical man like Beard, this new school of politics and economics. How exciting were Woodrow Wilson who studied how Congress actually worked rather than some theory of the separation of powers, or Frank Goodnow who had re-drafted the charter of New York City and took a radical view of *The Supreme Court and Social Reform* , his most memorable book. How exciting was Justice Holmes with his dictum that "The life of the law has not been logic, it has been experience," or Henry Demarest Lloyd who laid bare the anatomy and the pathology of the Standard Oil Company. It was all summed up by that other pioneer of modern studies, Charles E. Merriam of Chicago, who addressed himself to "the intimate study of the political processes dealing with interest groups and power practices, skills and understandings, forms of communication and personalities."

Beard was himself the first major American historian to bring pragmatism—or functionalism—to the interpretation of the past (and of the present as well). This was the guiding principle of his study of the Industrial Revolution, of the working of interest groups at the Constitutional Convention, of party battles in the Jeffersonian era, of the origins of judicial review; it permeated his vastly successful textbooks on American government and politics and his more specialized studies on the initiative and the referendum and on municipal administration. Like a good pragmatist, Beard kept his eye on the operation and the functioning of political institutions (and of judicial and economic institutions as well). Even in his unfortunate forays into foreign policy in the last decade of his life he used, or tried to use, the pragmatic approach; he rejected doctrines, spurned moral assumptions (or tried to), and argued that wars were to be understood within the framework of economic interests and ambitions.

So powerful was Beard that he not only reflected his own time, even more he created the image that others were to reflect, and in nothing more than his scepticism, his fishy view of the pretensions of the past—or rather of historians of the past, his readiness to tear the stuffing out of shirts and remove halos from swollen heads. He delighted in puncturing popular illusions, exposing the fallacies of familiar interpretations; if, as often the case, the fallacies were relatively unimportant or irrelevant, he managed to magnify them so their exposure at least could be significant. History as it unrolled from the pages of his magisterial volumes appeared plain, homespun, and familiar, its grand passions and its pretensions deflated.

All this was welcomed by an age which made no great plans and found satisfaction in the spectacle of the miscarriage of the great plans in the past; an age eager to discover that emperors—and presidents as well—had no clothes. Beard reflected something of the disillusionment of his own age—that is of the age of the 20's and the early 30's, and he contributed richly to the creation of that mood. Yet it is a mistake to emphasize overmuch the iconoclastic quality of Beard's mind and character. He was indeed a sceptic, and with something of the iconoclast in him, but he was, even more, a philosopher who wanted results, a reformer interested in change and progress. Romantic in his faith in progress, he was pragmatic in his methods of achieving it. In this he was like his associates at Columbia, Dewey and Goodnow and Harlan Stone and Edward Lee Thorndike, confident that they could reconstruct on sounder foundations the society which they were belaboring.

For all his impatience with mere traditionalism—the traditionalism that made a religion of the Constitution and sages and saints of all the Founding Fathers—Beard was himself a traditionalist; for all his rejection of the romantic aura that surrounded so much of the Civil War he was philosophically rooted in Romanticism. In this he was one with his great contemporaries, Turner and Parrington. If we look away from the style and manner of Beard's writing to the assumptions that underlie it and the philosophy which permeates it, we can see that notwithstanding the parade of scientific method, the scepticism and toughness, Beard's concept of history was fundamentally moralistic and romantic.

In a broad way we can discern two persistent and overarching uses of history from the beginning of formal historical writing to our own time. The first, and incomparably the most influential and distinguished, is that which scholars associate with Dionysius of Halicarnassus—and everyone else with Bolingbroke—that history is philosophy teaching by examples. The second, which has had many champions and which was in the ascendance during most of the past century and is still enormously influential, is that which we associate with Ranke—history as the comprehensive and faithful reconstruction of the past.

According to the first—that which held the field during the whole of the Classical Age, and again since the dawn of the secular state in the 16th century—the purpose and end of history was to discover those great moral laws that man should know, and, knowing, obey. This was the search that sent 18th century historians and statesmen back to the ancient world, persuaded them to reflect on the rise and fall of empires, on the dangers of power, on the fickleness of the public, on the inestimable value of freedom. It was what enabled them to embrace the whole of history as a single study, and to draw moral lessons with confidence from every age and every people, and from every level of society as well—the primitive as well as the sophisticated. Thus, their school anticipated what we call cultural anthropology. All particular histories were like tributaries, carrying their sediment of truth and morality and pouring it into the mainstream of history, where the faithful historians could dredge it up.

It was this school that dominated American writing of history from Thomas Jefferson and John Adams down through Bancroft and Prescott and Parkman—though with Parkman we get anticipations of the second more scientific school, and in performance, certainly, he did anticipate that. It was, on the whole, the German trained historians of the post-Civil War years who brought in the Ranke philosophy—the "noble dream" (to use Beard's somewhat nostalgic phrase) that scholars could indeed reconstruct the past, and that this was an important, dignified, and elevated activity.

Most of the great historians at the turn of the century sat at the feet of Ranke and his disciples, and accepted the "noble dream": that they might, with diligence and scrupulous honesty, reconstruct some segment of the past. Thus Henry Adams (before he got philosophy, as it were) confessed the purpose, "to satisfy himself whether, by severest process of stating, with the least possible comment, such facts as seemed sure, in such order as seemed rigorously consequent, he could fix for a familiar moment a necessary sequence of human movement." Needless to say, he concluded that he couldn't, though he had done so in nine volumes. Thus, too, most of the academic historians who filled the posts of power in the major universities—many of them trained in Ranke's Germany—were now taking control of the profession of history away from the amateurs of the past.

Turner had not been trained in Germany but at that Johns Hopkins which first (with Henry Adams's Harvard) introduced the German seminar method. He was only a partial convert to the "noble dream" that Beard later described. Parrington—next in line chronologically of the great triumvirate, but last to present his magnum opus—had never been exposed to German seminars. He was, after all, trained in literature in so far as he was trained at all, and it was not to the Germans he looked but to scholars and amateurs like Leslie Stephen or Hippolyte Taine or the Dane, Georg Brandes, from whom he borrowed the title of *Main Currents of American Thought*.

Beard, to be sure, had been amply exposed to the Rankean ideal—at Oxford where a series of Regius professors (including that Bishop Stubbs whose impact on Beard has been absurdly exaggerated: to my mind he learned from Stubbs how not to study history) had tried to impose on students the axiom that history is indeed a science, neither more nor less. When Beard returned to Columbia University to write his thesis on the justice of the peace in England he could hear the same doctrine from the mighty Burgess and the Olympian Dunning. Clearly their faith in the science of history was not infectious, but we should remember after all, in their favor, that their demonstration of a happy marriage between history and politics <u>was</u> infectious and did influence Mr. Beard profoundly.

I do not propose to discuss here the nature or development of Beard's revolt against historicism. That has been amply documented elsewhere and he has documented it himself. He argued first that it was quite impossible to achieve anything like a science of history, for we do not know what are the "facts" of history; we cannot possibly resurrect one-thousandth of those facts; the facts we do recover do not arrange themselves in any meaningful fashion, but are a chaos out of which the historian attempts to bring some order; they do not and cannot "speak for themselves" but can speak only through the historian who has his own language and his own accent, and more important has his own philosophy, and therefore his own principle of selection.

But there is an even more sobering consideration, for as Beard said:

> If a science of history could be achieved, it would, like the science of celestial mechanics, make possible the calculable prediction of the future of history. It would bring the totality of historical occurences within a single field, and reveal the unfolding future to its last end, including all the apparent choices made, and to be made. It would be omniscience. The creator of it would possess the attributes ascribed by the theologians to God the future once revealed mankind would have nothing to do but await its doom.

Beard's solution of this problem (if indeed we can call it a solution) was no more satisfactory than that of the historicists whom he belabored. Let us recognize, said Beard, that all history is controlled by the frame of reference in the mind of the historian; that history, then, is subjective. Let the historian acknowledge his frame of reference—and his subjectivity—and let him frankly use history "to throw light on the quandaries of our day, and to facilitate adjustment and reform." In this sense all history would be contemporary history or even—what Jefferson had anticipated and what has not been adequately followed up—would be prospective rather than retrospective history. For if history exists chiefly in the mind of the historian (or as Jefferson assumed, in the imagination of the historian) then the past that the historian sees is merely a contemporary view of the past. History then would be obliged to use the past to understand and direct the future.

What do we have here but a more sophisticated version of the ancient principle that history is philosophy teaching by examples? Inevitably this view leads to a now familiar vulgarization of history—the requirement that history must be relevant, and indeed we may add that if all history is contemporary history then whatever history is studied is *per se* relevant because all that is contemporary is presumably relevant—which gets very confusing. Beard—like Croce and Dilthey, whom he admired—was far more sophisticated about this than many of our contemporaries, especially the young, and did not himself yield too uncritically to the demands of history as edification or history as relevance. But his ultimate purpose was not very different from that which animated the historians of the ancient world like Thucydides or Tacitus or Polybius or those of the Enlightenment like Voltaire and Montesquieu, Gibbon or Hume.

Nowhere is the historical romanticism of the great triumvirate of Turner, Parrington, and Beard more interesting than in their reflection of what we have come to call "consensus" history (a very new term) and their emphasis on conflict. There was of course awareness of conflict in the historians of the 19th century—most notably, perhaps, in Henry Adams himself, who was a great transition figure. But there can be no doubt that the underlying theme was unity. For the 19th century—not perhaps among historians alone—was fascinated (with good cause) by the spectacle of the ability of the United States to remain one nation (and the history of the Civil War was written pretty much in terms of single nationalism, not of dual nationalism), to avoid revolution, to eliminate class distinctions among whites, to free the slaves and to provide legal equality of the races, to lift standards of living, to function as a melting pot, to avoid religious conflicts and war, and so forth. After all, most of the American historians had been trained on the history of the ancient world, the history of England, and of the European continent. No wonder they were bemused, even dazzled, that their own country had somehow avoided the evils and perils that had afflicted the nations of the Old World and had, almost miraculously, created unity out of variety. It was not surprising that they should read, in the mottoes which the Founding Fathers had provided with almost Providential wisdom: *E pluribus unum* and *Novus ordo saeclorum*, a Providential prophecy.

It is with Turner, Parrington, and Beard that we get the decisive swing from consensus history to history which is more interested in division, contrast, and conflict than in what they came to see as merely surface unity. That new awareness was not so decided in Turner as in his two contemporaries, for though Turner did, indeed, concentrate on sectionalism, he did, at the same time, concentrate on the great force that promised unity: the frontier, open land, and all that these symbolize in distinguishing the New World from the Old and in forming an American democracy and an American character distinct from the politics and character of Europe.

This new school continued the romanticism of its predecessor and added a parochialism heretofore absent. What has emerged in the past few decades might be called neither consensus nor conflict but complexity. Yet our current preoccupation with complexity carries with it a curious kind of simplification: we are so busy today analyzing newly-detected complexities in our society that we tend to ignore (or simply have no time for) the vastly greater complexities of a hemispheric or a global character. Because scholars concentrate so heavily on the domestic and even the local scene, they almost inevitably exaggerate every variation on a familiar theme, and they sometimes ignore those differences between Old World and New which—if recognized—would emphasize not so much complexity and conflict in our own history as simplicity and unity. Concentration on conflict and complexity is certainly justified in that arena of which Professor Genovese is the acknowledged master, and now at last we are studying slavery for almost the first time not just as a local or national phenomenon but as a world phenomenon.

One explanation of our growing preoccupation with conflict and complexity is that modern tools of research, notably the computer, greatly facilitate the discovery of distinctions. Historians have always known that the first principle of research was to count and to measure. Only now, perhaps, are they able so to measure large areas of history, vast ranges of historical activities, an infinite body of raw materials, that they can approximate a science of history. Bemused, now by the potentialities of new tools, historians are tempted to measure everything, and just as by all physical measurements, every human being is greatly different from all others and is indeed unique, and it is the differences that are ostentatious, so measurement brings home to us awareness that every community, every ethnic group, every political, economic, religious interest is profoundly different from every other and is indeed unique. Now common sense had suggested these differences to the past and common sense told us, too, that all these differences in societies, as in men and women, could be taken for granted, and that different individuals, churches, unions, etc., did after all have common denominators which enabled them to live together most of the time. This was one of the great fundamental principles of the Enlightenment, the principle of universality: by nature men were everywhere the same, said the Enlightment, and philosophers could safely draw upon the experience of every people, from remote antiquity, distant climes, and different civilizations for illustrations. You could learn from China, from Tahiti, from the Indians, from the Vikings: from the remote past and the immediate present. Thus, for example, the passion for nudity which characterized the 18th century art was absolutely logical: take the clothes off and all human beings are alike. "My God," said the young Benjamin West, when he was first shown the Apollo Belvedere by his enraptured host, "how like a Mohawk Indian." It is romanticism, of course, that clothed people, for as soon as you put clothes on, you know whether you are dealing with a Greek or a Viking or an Indian, a nobleman or a peasant. It is nudity that universalizes mankind, clothing that fragments it.

But now — curiously enough just at a time when an all but global technology does permit a certain standardization — it is the differences that fascinate us, both in the past and in the present.

Beard saw a conflict — either of interest or of integrity — between a life of scholarship and a life of public service. His first book, *The History of the Industrial Revolution*, was a product of his interest in the education of workingmen in England, and thereafter he was ceaselessly active in public as in academic affairs. He taught constitutional history and government, and wrote on the initiative and referendum, and was a guiding spirit in the New York City Bureau of Municipal Research. His interests and activities flowed into each other adding force and strength to each other. He wrote for fellow scholars, for learned magazines, for journals of opinion, on broad public issues and for a broad public. *The Republic* sold something like four million copies, his text books sold additional millions. He was, without a doubt, the most widely read American historian of his day, and perhaps of any day: how astonishing that he was the most influential figure among professional historians — probably among professional political scientists as well! He did not regard "popularity" as a stigma, but as a fulfillment and a proper recognition of his work.

Now let us turn to Beard and his contemporaries from another point of view. If we look at the history of the concept of uniqueness—and not in the realm of historical writing alone but in its larger political, social, and philosophical implications—we can see that it derives from and responds to environment. The generation of the Founding Fathers had a different—perhaps more inclusive word for it—climate; all of them were environmentalists or students of climate. Climate embraced not just land and weather, flora and fauna: it embraced government, religion, morals, and a host of other social institutions. It was climate that reassured the generation of the Founding Fathers that America need not be bound by the experience of the past but—in this new and more nearly perfect environment—could write a new page in history.

All three of the great progressive historians were environmentalists and were therefore heirs to the 18th and 19th century view of history. Turner was the simplest of the environmentalists. To him environment was open land, a frontier, sectional differences; Turner's disciples, like Walter Webb, John Hicks, Everett Dick and J.C. Malin, refined on the Turner environmental interpretation; but none of these, except Webb in his very last book, studied the frontier in a global framework as a phenomenon, not only of American, but of Canadian, Australian, African, Russian and Chinese history. That remained for a geographer, Isaiah Bowman. Parrington, steeped though he was in the history of European literature and architecture, was likewise an environmentalist and intellectually an isolationist; only rarely did he project his story of American liberal thought outside the boundaries of the United States, and when he did, it was commonly for just that kind of contrast which Jefferson had made when he expatiated on New World innocence and Old World depravity. So eager was Parrington to contrast the forces of darkness and the forces of light that struggled for dominance over the American soul, that he greatly exaggerated the differences between the various American schools. Jefferson and Hamilton were indeed far apart, and so were John Adams and Benjamin Franklin. But contrast Jefferson with Edmund Burke and Adams with Voltaire, contrast Franklin with Count Bernstorff, and Hamilton with Count Struensee and you must conclude that what united American revolutionary leaders was far more important than what divided them. Parrington was more sensitive than Turner or Beard to the European inheritance which was to be transformed into an American culture. Yet though he could not fail to recognize the American debt to that inheritance, what interested him was the revolt against it in the United States and the transformation of it into something new, and, what was more important, into something better. "Transplanted to American soil," he wrote, "these seedlings (of philosophy) from the Old World nurseries took root and flourished in such spots as proved congenial, stimulating American thought, suggesting programs for fresh utopian ventures, providing an intellectual sanction for new experiments in government. They gave impulse and form to our native idealisms and contributed largely to the outcome of our social experience. The child of two continents, America can be explained in its significant traits by neither alone." "Intellectual sanction for new experiments in government..." said Parrington—that is something that Beard on the whole missed, or if he did not miss it (for he did not miss very much), something he chose to dismiss...and of course if you look at history through economic glasses, you cannot be greatly distracted by intellectual sanctions. Beard was more concerned, after all, with economic sanctions, social and class sanctions, political sanctions. Only in one of his last books, *The American Spirit,* did he address himself to intellectual origins—that is the Old World origins—of American ideas and institutions. His analysis was not systematic but narrative, impressionistic and tumultuous.

Beard's environmentalism was closer to that of Thomas Jefferson, oddly enough, than it was to that of his contemporaries Turner or Parrington. It was geographic— not in an elementary physiographic sense, but in a larger political sense, for to Beard the importance of American geography inhered in the isolation of America from Europe, and in its economic self-sufficiency. It was political, for notwithstanding Beard's sophistication about British and other forms of parliamentary government, he preferred the American. It was economic for he was a "Continentalist"—did he borrow that term from Alexander Hamilton who was probably the first one to use it?—confident that we could get along very well without European trade, European influences even. It was—here the debt to Jefferson is particularly suggestive—moral, for like Jefferson, Beard was prepared to build a wall of fire between the corruptions of the Old World and the innocence of the New.

But this was merely the most ostentatious of Beard's many parodoxes, one which Beard would have embraced with a cheerful reminder from Ralph Waldo Emerson that "A foolish consistency is the hobgoblin of little minds." How indeed could a scholar who wrote indefatigably on so many subjects—one rapt critic has totalled it up for us: eight volumes on European history, twenty-one volumes of American history, fifteen textbooks, a total here of 21,000 pages and in addition, no doubt another twenty thousand pages or so of articles and reviews—how could so prolific a scholar be held to some standard of consistency over a period of 40 or 50 years? Was it paradoxical that the most philosophical of our historians (excluding Henry Adams who developed his philosophy after he wrote history) should have formulated a philosophy of history that repudiated existing philosophies and concluded that history is after all an act of faith and is not faith a way of doing without philosophy? Was it paradoxical that the most nearly cosmopolitan of our modern historians should end up as the champion of isolation and on a note that celebrated parochialism? Was it paradoxical that the scholar who scorned the myths, the fallacies, and the humbug of the past and who specifically repudiated what he called the devil theory of history, should himself have confessed an irresistible penchant for the conspiracy theory of history and should have given comfort and respectability to those who were delighted to think that the Constitution was itself a conspiracy, that the Fourteenth Amendment was the product of a conspiracy, and that Franklin Roosevelt filled very well the position of devil when it came to explaining our entry into the second world war?

Is there a further paradox in Beard's combination of the realistic and the romantic in history? We think of Beard as the very symbol of the modern, even the scientific, historian (and this though he rejected the possibility of history being truly scientific), but in his readiness to use history to point a moral, he was one with the Classicists and the Romantics, and so too in his confidence that environment accounted for the unique American civilization. Elsewhere, too, he was animated by ideas we associate chiefly with Romanticism. Nowhere is this more arresting than in his fascination with nationalism and with the ideas of national interest and national character.

Nationalism is the political form of Romanticism, as Romanticism is the literary and cultural form of nationalism. The Enlightenment was essentially cosmopolitan and international—an era when the claims of class or of cultural allegiance took precedence over the claims of nationalism, when wars were fought, as often as not, by mercenaries, when an American could be prime minister of Bavaria and when an Englishman was prime minister of Naples, when the Royal Academy conferred its gold medal on Franklin even as Britain was at war with the rebellious colonies, and the French Academy conferred its gold medal on Humphrey Davy in the midst of the Napoleonic Wars, and the great Dr. Jenner could write that "The sciences are never at war," and be right. Modern nationalism can be dated from the American and the French Revolutions, and both brought with them an insistence on prior claims of national loyalties and on the dignity of national cultures. Beard could assume a sardonic attitude toward the pretensions and the frauds of the past, but he was in truth dissembling his love even as he kicked his historical characters down the stairs. He was in fact not only an ardent patriot, but an ardent nationalist, confident of American superiority in material and practical matters, and in cultural as well. In this he was at one with both Turner and Parrington, for he shared their conviction that there was indeed an American character and an American mind: the overall title of Beard's four-volume survey of American history was the *Rise of American Civilization*, and the final volume rejoiced in the title *The American Spirit*. Nor did he rationalize the concept of a distinctive American civilization by a resort to cultural anthropology as had some of the philosophers of the Enlightenment, who invented that subject. No, American uniqueness was social, it was political, it was—increasingly he moved to this view—moral. Odd that Beard's deep concern for the moral aspects of American civilization should have ended with a passionate crusade for America standing aloof from the greatest moral crisis of modern history.

There was logic in Turner's theory of uniqueness and emphasis upon it. After all, it could be said that the American experience with an open frontier for over 200 years, and with the problem of accomodating a European inheritance to a primitive environment was indeed unique. But Beard concerned himself rather with the Industrial Revolution, the factory system, class conflict, the city, technology, capitalism and corporations—with all of those major interests which were precisely not unique but general and almost global—institutions which had for the most part developed in the Old World, and whose Old World development would, presumably, throw a great deal of light on their development in the New. No one knew this better than the Beard who had written in his first book on the Industrial Revolution, and who was familiar with the governments and economies of many foreign nations not only in Europe but in the Far East as well, and an expert in comparative constitutional law and comparative economic history; the Beard, we may add, who was at home in not only German history and economics, but even in German historical philosophy.

Yet in the face of all this familiarity with the history of the Old World, Beard clung tenaciously to the assumption—mostly implicit but occasionally explicit—that the American scene was different, almost unique, and so too the American spirit. And if it was not, it ought to be. He might have said what Tocqueville said, but in reverse: In Europe I see more than Europe, I see the future of America. And as Tocqueville studied the New World in order to help France avoid its errors and calamities, so Beard called upon his countrymen to take well to heart the history and the character of the Old World that we might protect ourselves against it and immunize ourselves from it or to it.

There was a paradoxical quality inherent in Beard's deliberate parochialism—the paradoxical quality which we find in so much of the environmental and the conflict school of history, namely, that intense concentration on the American scene tended to exaggerate differences and conflicts, and to blind students to what was new and original. It is this, I think that is at the root of the difficulty with the *Economic Interpretation of the Constitution* —not merely that modern scholarship has shot the argument full of holes; not merely that Beard himself came, if not to doubt it, then to discard it. It was rather the failure to see how really remarkable was the achievement at Philadelphia in 1787; a failure, that is, to consider (either in this book or in his *Rise of American Civilization*) the astonishing achievement of federalism—the first successful federal system in history—or of the new colonial policy—the first solution of colonialism in history—or to appreciate the phenomenon—very much in the minds of Madison and Wilson and others—of a people making their own government. This permitted Beard the luxury of arguing (I think mistakenly) that the writing and ratification of the Constitution was a *coup d'etat*. It encouraged him to concentrate on the limited nature of public support—as revealed in such statistics of voting as were then available—when in fact the astounding thing was the spectacle of any government having any formal public support at all in the 18th century world: shades of Louis XV or Frederick the Great, or for that matter, of George III! It permitted him to all but ignore the achievement of religious liberty and the separation of church and state, which he simply took for granted. We still rather take these things for granted, though our religious scene is still most extraordinary; we have a situation, almost unique in the modern world for the last 200 years, where it is possible for a man deeply orthodox in religion, to be mildly radical in politics, like Bryan, or for a Catholic like Kennedy to carry through a revolution and for a Unitarian like Taft to be deeply conservative in politics and where else but in the United States would an agnostic like Robert Ingersoll be able to place in nomination for the Presidency a reactionary like James G. Blaine!

This environmentalist approach which seemed to exclude a comparative one, characterized Beard's work throughout most of his fantastically productive career. The isolationism of the final years was not just a feeling that all wars did more harm than good (something he would not in fact, have said of the American Revolution) nor a reaction to his conviction that Wilson had tricked the nation into the first world war, nor even a manifestation of his deep distrust of Franklin D. Roosevelt. It went deeper than all this; its intellectual and moral roots were to be found in that Jefferson whom Beard rather distrusted; in the conviction that while totalitarianism might indeed threaten nations and peoples of the Old World, it was still none of our concern, because the Old World was beyond redemption and must be allowed to stagger to its doom in its own way. No American of his generation was more alert to threats against freedom, or more responsive to the call for the defense of freedom on the domestic scene, than Charles A. Beard. But, he did not think that European freedom was worth imperilling American integrity. He was confident that America was so strong, so self-sufficient (morally as well as economically) that she need not fear the triumph of totalitarianism abroad.

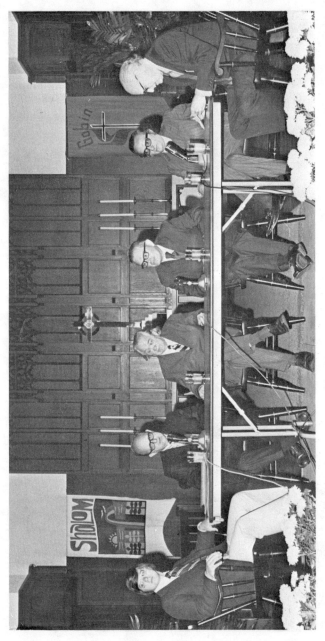

Panel discussion participants were (left to right) Ripley Tilden, DePauw University senior history majors' representative; Dr. John Braeman; Dr. Henry Steele Commager; Dr. John Baughman; Dr. Eugene Genovese; and Dr. Clifton Phillips.

Panel Discussion

John Wilson: I would now like to introduce the panel. Our distinguished historians have already been introduced, but I will very briefly indicate them again. Next to the end on our right is Professor Eugene Genovese of the University of Rochester, who spoke yesterday afternoon on Charles Beard and the Economic Interpretation of History. On the left and next to the end, Dr. John Braeman of the University of Nebraska, who spoke last evening on the topic, Charles A. Beard: Historian and Progressive, Professor Commager we have already introduced this morning and the rest of the panel are all from DePauw. On the far end is Professor Clifton Phillips whose field is both Asia and U.S. History but he has a special interest in Charles Beard and at the opposite end, Mr. Charles Tilden who is the senior history majors' representative and a history and English major. Moderating the panel is Dr. John Baughman whose field is European History but he bears the distinction of being the only Hoosier in the Department.

John Baughman: Thank you. We determined our procedure last night for the panel as one in which each of us will speak a few momemts and then enter into debate. Our guests very kindly suggested that the non-participants so far in the program lead off today and we appreciate this gesture. First, we would like to have a few words from Professor Phillips.

Clifton Phillips: Thank you. We've all listened with great pleasure, I know, to the very rich fare that we have had here yesterday and today and I must confess I feel somewhat at a loss to make a comment or a few comments on all of them that would somehow bring together a synthesis here in my own thinking about Charles Beard, but I'd like to set forth two or three points that have come to my mind as I have listened to these three addresses and that relate in particular to what I know best about Beard, that is to say, his background in Indiana and at DePauw.

First of all, I would begin where Professor Commager began with Charles Beard as a son of the Middle Border, and stress the midwestern flavor and special midwestern quality of his life and work, indeed his Hoosier flavor. Here I speak not as a native Hoosier but one who was transplanted to this heartland of America twenty years ago and have learned, perhaps, some sensitivity to the midwestern nuance which, I think, can be seen in Charles Beard's writings and in his life style. I don't speak here of what has often been pointed out as Charles Beard as a lecturer at Columbia and elsewhere, with the midwestern drawl, the, perhaps, somewhat sardonic humor associated often with the Middle West but, in particular, I would stress what he got from his first twenty-four years—what might be called his formative experience here in Indiana and I would stress the nationalist quality as Professor Commager did in his address.

Charles Beard's father came from North Carolina just at the outset of the Civil War in order to remain loyal to the national union. In fact, he just avoided being mobilized into the Confederate forces. Charles Beard grew up in an

Indiana that was very much influenced by the great impact of the Civil War which was seen here, of course, not as an ideological struggle at all but as a struggle for national unity. It is the special midwestern quality of nationalism that Professor Braeman has associated, of course, with another of DePauw's alumni, Senator Albert Beveridge. I would say Beveridge and Beard both belonged to what might be called the Nationalist Wing of Progressivism as opposed to the Internationalist Eastern Seaboard Wing, despite the fact that Charles Beard and Mary Beard shook the dust of Indiana from them rather impatiently as they left DePauw at the turn of the century and went first to England and then to New York City where they resided together with their summer home in Connecticut for the rest of their lives. A good deal of midwestern qualities still persisted in both Charles and Mary. Charles always said that he was raised in the Federalist Whig Republican tradition which particularly in eastern Indiana was the post-Civil War syndrome there.

Another element I would put with this would be the Evangelical component. This aspect has not been spoken of by any of our speakers directly, for example, Beard's Quaker background, his Methodist experience here at DePauw, and his activity in the Temperance Movement. He spoke to many working men's temperance unions in the black industrial midlands of England. He was a Prohibitionist figure as was Mary Ritter. The Ritter family, too, was associated with the Prohibitionist movement. Although Beard lost a good deal of the particularly theological quality of Evangelicalism, he maintained a secularized version and remained an Evangelist, a preacher of a gospel of secular progress and in particular of American progress that I think helped explain the paeans to American democracy of which both Professor Braeman and Professor Commager have spoken.

Parenthetically, I think it is interesting to note how large a part middle westerners played in the intellectual reform movement of the early twentieth century. Such a New

York institution as the New School for Social Research, which three of our speakers mentioned, was founded, of course, not by a single native New Yorker but by four backtrailers from the Middle Border as Hamlin Garlan would have called them: by Alvin Johnson from Nebraska, Thorstein Veblen from Wisconsin, James Harvey Robinson from Iowa and Charles Austin Beard from Indiana. Not a native Easterner among them and it was conducted by those transplanted midwesterners during much of its early history.

On the question of conflict and consensus, Charles Beard again is a true son of the Middle Border, with the Civil War having a great impact. He saw contradictions in American society as being in a good Marxist term as Chairman Mao likes to say "non-antagonistic contradictions," and the only possible contradiction in American society which seemed insoluble was, of course, slavery, and Charles Beard finally brought the economic interpretation to this. This was simply a clash of economic interests which had to be resolved by resorting to war, which certainly is not simply a resolution of economic terms. But I think this is the way Indianans and this is the way midwesterners looked upon the national unity, and the only clashes that took place were resolvable clashes.

Charles Beard then was kind of a consensus historian who saw the conflicts as a non-antagonistic contradiction within the particular American system with its great genius for overcoming these kinds of contradictions in our constitutional system. The Charles Beard interest in American civilization which Professor Commager stressed so greatly towards the end of his address, too, I think was the reason why Charles Beard did not develop a general theory of economic or historical development, and his economic interpretation of history was not meant to be such a general theory because he was not a comparativist. As a manner of fact, few historians were. I suppose Francis Parkman came as close with his study of French and English colonization in America, and, of course, saw the

French seigneurial system as different from the British colonial system, but most American historians have not been comparativists. It's only today that the comparative approach is being made. Charles Beard, I think Professor Commager has well said, despite his early interest in England and European history and his work there, published works in which he saw America as the basic unit of his historical studies and did not make the kind of comparative analysis that would have been necessary to produce a truly general theory of historical development.

Charles Tilden: I think I must pick up Dr. Phillips' theme because all three professors who spoke alluded to or touched upon a speech that Charles Beard gave in 1933 to the American Historical Association regarding history as an act of faith. This is, of course, what Professor Braeman discussed quite well last night and the key point of that was that any selection and arrangement of facts pertaining to any area of history is controlled by the frame of reference in the mind of the historian. This is something that was touched on by Professor Commager this morning. And, in that sense, if we consider, as Mr. Vagts did last night at the dinner banquet, the background of Charles Beard, I would have to agree with Dr. Phillips that indeed Beard had no intention of becoming a comparative historian. It was mentioned this morning by Professor Commager that we get the great interest in history by looking at the divisions of various groups. I found that quite interesting because if you consider the period in which Beard wrote you see there was indeed a great deal of division beneath the surface and I think that will add a bit of light as to why Beard attacked the superficial unity approach and moved to look at history beneath the surface. As a result, that brings me to what Mr. Genovese had to say yesterday afternoon, and that was that Beard was not able to deal with psychological factors because Beard's main emphasis was on economics. But, I wonder, as I think about it, judging from the context in which Beard spoke and wrote, isn't it perhaps the case that Beard was able to go beneath the surface and look at divisions in history—might not that include psychological factors? I hope we will have an opportunity to discuss that in the coming minutes.

Eugene Genovese: The point I was driving at was not at all that Beard was insensible to the complexities of psychology in history. He certainly wrestled with this problem, and particularly, with what might not very accurately be called a political psychology. What I was driving at was something a bit different. That is, if we look at that part of his work which reflected his efforts at economic interpretation and recall that he defined his categories as interest groups, I can see no starting point there for a coherent approach to the psychological dimension of the struggles he was portraying. I tried to suggest that it would have been quite different if, when he spoke of classes, he meant classes rather than interest groups, because in that instance he would have had to face the psychological dimension of the way in which human beings confront each other in their social relations. For example, if I were to approach the question of the psychological dimension of the slave experience and its relationship, let us say, to the way in which the southerners shaped their policies in the 50's, even their rhetoric and the extreme violence with which they approached certain questions—indeed, they have been accused of paranoia but I don't go along with that—I should say that an attack on the psychological dimension there would have to begin with their fundamental relationship to their slaves, to what the existence of lordship and bondage meant on that human level. When

Beard attacked these problems in terms of economic interpretation, he was talking about interest groups facing each other in market relations, and so on. He illuminated much about the economic dimension of the struggle, but I don't think you can construct coherent social psychology on that foundation; and I think that Beard, himself, backed away from it very quickly.

John Braeman: One of the central themes of the remarks here and in general writings on Beard — and Mr. Commager has made a great point of this — seems to be the paradoxes in Beard's thinking. I am not really convinced that the paradoxes are as paradoxical as they seem. One thing, I hate to be historical about it, but I think one has to trace Beard's development in the chronological framework, that his ideas changed over time in response to reading, to his own experiences. He was a man who had what is rare in the academy, the ability to learn, not merely from reading other academicians but learning from experiences. There is no question that his ideas and emphases and stresses changed over time. For instance, on the point of Beard the nationalist, isolationist, or continentalist, at the time of World War I he was, as early as the Lusitania crisis, an ardent interventionist. He was a strong supporter of American membership in an international organization. The League of Nations wasn't even quite strong enough for him. He was for one of the world government type of things, and his views on that changed quite dramatically as the result of experiences that he had largely in the 20's and the 30's. So, I would suggest that thinking in terms of development and change is a good deal more important in trying to deal with Beard than trying to pick out paradoxes in his thought.

Baughman: Prof. Commager, would you care to comment?

Henry Commager: I am struck by what both Professors Phillips and Genovese said. I do not wish to comment directly on that, but how interesting it is that the last time we had a comparative approach to history, was the era of the Enlightenment. Perhaps it was Mr. Jefferson after all who did know what slavery did to the tempers of men. He said at one time the institution of slavery was a perpetual invitation to the exercise of the most boisterous of passions, and he deplored slavery for what it did to the whites as well as what it did to the blacks. The 18th century did have a comparative sense of history. That comparison was not so much with modern European but with ancient history. John Adams wrote three ponderous and impossible volumes drawing on the experience of some fifty-eight different quasi-republics over the long stretch of history and all, of course, proving the same thing, that man was corrupt and depraved and must be saved from himself by checks, balances, limitations and everything else Adams could think of. The forefathers were familiar with the history of England, above all with the work of the 17th and 18th century Commonwealth men. Adams' discourses on Davila were discourses on a 16th-17th century French historian. Somewhere along the line, possibly with the passing of classical education, we lost the comparative view of the past and I think it is important to resurrect it, not necessarily with respect to Greek and Roman history but with the European past, if we are to appreciate the significance of the American experiment.

Braeman: I would argue that Beard knew

more about comparative history than anybody of his time.

Commager: You are right, but he didn't use it!

Braeman: I would say that he would argue quite to the contrary, that he did use it and that it led him to the conclusion that America was basically different.

Commager: That is the conclusion that Adams and Jefferson had come to. Because the Old World was basically evil, because it had made nothing but mistakes, it had staggered from calamity to disaster, from disaster to catastrophe over the ages. The only thing to do was to build a wall of fire between the Old World and the New. Now this was not the younger Beard—the Beard who created Ruskin College. Beard did change. The paradoxes are not those of any moment. They persist over a long and enormously active period of historical interpretation and they appear more sharply to our day than they did to his day because we look at the whole corpus of Beard's work and see these seeming contradictions within it. They are understandable if we follow the career through from 1901 to 1948.

Genovese: I wonder if I might ask my colleagues to develop one of the criticisms that they seem to agree on and that is that Beard made a mess out of his political position on the eve of the second world war. I am struck by this, not because I sympathize with Beard's isolationism at that period at all, but I think it does pose a problem as to what the relationship was of his politics and his very passionate involvement and the way he was reading history. Mr. Commager suggested this morning, and again just now, that he was ready to write off Europe, as it were. But the question I would really like to put to you, gentlemen, is this, if I can phrase it sharply: You admire certain aspects of Beard's work that I have more reservations about, namely what you both call his pragmatism and his turning away from what might be called a general theory of history. But I do wonder how or why we should not appreciate above everything else the way in which Beard, having that commitment, I would say philosophical commitment (though I know pragmatists like to think it is a way of doing without a philosophy), and reading the European experience in the way he did, at the same time became appalled by the drift of the United States into war. It seems to me that what lent particular passion to his polemics was the sense that the American people were not being told "this is a moral struggle you should be engaged in," but on the contrary were being deceived and lied to. This adds up, it seems to me, to be a consistent package and one which one might argue ended in a political error. But I do think that it flowed much more firmly from the very attitudes toward history that particularly Professors Commager and Braeman seem most to admire in him. And, I would think, perhaps, that this is the paradox in Beard, if it is a paradox, that you have to confront because perhaps it suggests a paradox in the way in which you evaluate his work.

Commager: I agree with what you said: the paradox could be put philosophically — though Beard didn't really like the term. Anyway, I tried to put it that while his method was pragmatic, his philosophy was, in many ways, that of the 18th or early 19th century—history as philosophy teaching by examples. He was a moralist all his life but there is a deep problem here. Perhaps we simply don't have the evidence to resolve it. I wish Beard's children and grandchildren who knew him so well, would clarify this for us: to what extent did he see the rise of Hitler, the Spanish Civil War, things of that kind in moral terms? The younger Beard would have seen these questions in moral terms. He saw World War I in moral terms. Most of my colleagues at Columbia had known Mr. Beard as a colleague. They told how outraged he was at German militarism, how he paced the corridors of Fayerweather Hall, calling on his colleagues to work for intervention; how impatient he was with Wilson for his delays, and for the way he seemed to play politics with this issue, and so forth. But I have no feeling from the evidence we have, (we don't have the right kind of evidence) that after the mid 30's on Beard, who had been so concerned with the fate of foreign scholars in the 20's and early thirties, was so deeply upset by Hitler's threat to civilization and morality that he could balance that against his fear of what might happen to America if she got involved in the war. We don't know if he was in favor of some kind of intervention in the Spanish Civil War which was one of the great turning points of modern history and of history as morality. On the record I find little evidence that he allowed such moral considerations to influence his political judgments.

Braeman: On the specific point of the Spanish Civil War he did, in fact, in magazine articles, criticize the American embargo as an unneutral act. And there is abundant evidence that he did feel great moral revulsion against Hitler and Hitlerism. But I think there were several countervailing things at work here. First of all, he didn't have very great respect for the so-called democracies of Europe. As he said in a magazine article, his trouble was that he could not see much moral superiority in Britain, France, or Russia as compared with Germany. And Matthew Josephson reports a conversation that Beard had with, I think, the French novelist Louis Aragon, in which Beard declaimed about how Britain and France were the most ruthless of imperialist powers and thus wherefore were they any better than Hitler's Germany. I think he basically thought they were better. But, on the other hand, he feared that war would mean the end of reform in America, the destruction of civil liberties, and a long train of unhappy consequences. As he wrote to H.L. Mencken, he had no illusions about Hitler's peaceable intentions toward the United States. In the 1930's he even favored universal military training as a means of national defense. But he assumed, and this was another act of faith (you will find this in his testimony before congressional committees on rearmament proposals), that the United States was impregnable, that the oceans would preserve it.

Professor Genovese's point, I think, is well taken. I agree that there is a coherence, a unity, between Beard's views on foreign and domestic policy. This is most strikingly shown in his beliefs that American involvement in World War II had come about because of the domestic failures of the New Deal. From the start, he had worried that Roosevelt would try to solve the Depression by seeking markets abroad and that this would bring us into conflict, particularly with Japan. But as the European crisis worsened, this argument did not seem to him to be applicable to that situation and he did eventually succumb to a devil theory of Roosevelt. That is, to the view that Roosevelt was, to a large extent, seeking to divert the American people from his own domestic failures by leading them off to foreign adventures. So there is this basic coherence, basic unity, in the two sides of Beard.

Commager: I'm more and more impressed, (if I may just put in a footnote) by the analogy to Jefferson. Jefferson had the same passion for domestic reform, the same feeling that America was incomparably superior to all other things and therefore for all of his enormous cosmopolitanism (he was happier in Paris than anywhere else), he was prepared to cut himself off completely from the Old World because the Old World might infect the New with its depravity. The curious thing is (maybe this is another paradox, so I won't over-emphasize it) that Beard didn't really like Jefferson very much either. It's rather odd that *The American Spirit* gives six pages to Jefferson, twelve to Barlow, and I think sixteen to a rather forgotten character named Robert Coram—who was a pretty good educator in his way—Jefferson himself gets very short shrift in that book. Beard wasn't psychologically at home with Jefferson, in a way he was psychologically more at home with Madison and Hamilton than he was with Jefferson. Nevertheless, he did share the Jeffersonian philosophy of isolationism, even though he had not quite Jefferson's cosmopolitanism though he had a great deal of it.

Genovese: I think I would like to press a little further because I do think we have some differences obscured in all this agreement. You see, one of the things that troubles me about the discussion so far and one of the things that I particularly respect about the way it seems to me that Beard struggled with the great moral issue of the time is that I have difficulty understanding how one can take a historical view of politics and at the same time maintain a moralistic view. Except on two premises: first, if there is a deep commitment to revere God. But if this is to be done historically, I would think that it can only make sense if that commitment is read into the historical record, that is to say, if there was a theological conception of history. Alternatively, there must be a commitment to a theory of historical process which carries with it its own moral judgments, for if not, the type of thing you were talking about, Mr. Commager, when you spoke about history as moral example, etc., ultimately does become subjective and arbitrary. I think Beard was very conscious of the dangers in that, although I agree with you in saying that he comes very much out of that tradition and that his own work should be understood that way. Now, it seems to me, therefore, that this willingness to impose his own moral judgment and, indeed, moral revulsion against Hitler or even, as Mr. Braeman pointed out last night, in relation to the Soviet Union, represented an awareness on his part that without a general theory of history, which he rejected out of his pragmatism, and without a theological conception, he had, in fact, no right to impose his morality understand what was going on within him at all, that his attitude suggests not merely paradox but an almost tragic confrontation in his own life's work. But I do not think that it represents a very tough-minded way of dealing with the problems of a pragmatic view of history.

Baughman: Mr. Phillips, would you care to comment?

Phillips: One comment there that strikes me is that perhaps Beard's historicism is at the root of this problem in part. That this perhaps explains the problem that Professor Genovese has raised here. The basis for Beard's judgment, his moral judgment in particular, was that he was, until his later pessimism, an historicist, as Professor Commager said, who believed that history had a saving grace and that history would save, that scientific history would save us, and that there was a movement in history that was going forward toward an ultimate end. He lost this view, of course, in his reading of German historigraphical writings in the 30's, although he did make an act of faith as he said (as all historians have to do), and he made the leap of faith that there is such a movement. I think that replaced perhaps the general theory of history for him. It's kind of a rather naive historicism.

Commager: I suspect Beard like so many others, and of course my distinguished colleagues, tried to separate his historical philosophy with its rigorous requirements of objectivity and its misgivings about making moral judgment, from his private and personal life and his passionate involvement in the affairs of his own and other countries. It is very hard to speak as an historian in the morning and then go down to Washington and try to change things, or write for popular magazines—and Beard wrote hundreds if not thousands of articles designed to influence current affairs—and keep that Olympian historical view. Indeed, Beard himself said that no one could do it. Why pretend you can be Olympian; all history is after all subjective. He tried his best, I believe, to distinguish these things but allowed himself inevitably to get deeply involved. In the last few books he went I think too far to demonstrate that history is subjective.

Tilden: Isn't this really asking too much of Beard, for that matter of any human being, to not come up with some kind of moral judgment, particularly in the context of the build-up of World War II? Don't you think that would be asking too much of Beard to remove his own opinions from that build-up?

Commager: His moral judgment was that we shouldn't have moral judgments. After all it was, he in effect said look at British history, look at Russian history, look at French history, all nations go through this; he might have added look at American history, look what we did to the Indians, look what we did to the blacks; nations, like people, are all great sinners, fundamentally corrupt. Let us not therefore, separate the saved and the damned, let us not look at the Old World to say that Hitler is irremediably evil, after all Napoleon was evil, so many people have been evil and mankind has survived. We can sit this one out, we are impregnable, we are safe, we are guardians of civilization. After all, here in America the great ideals of the past have found a refuge, the experiment in democracy has been carried forward; this evil will pass as other great wars have passed, it will not in fact destroy civilization. Therefore it is better to save America and let it be the instrument of regenerating the world than to plunge in ourselves, be contaminated and destroyed as we will be destroyed morally by war. Remember all this is pre-atomic-bomb reasoning! That I think was the way he read it.

Braeman: There's just one thing I would like to toss in here and that is when you read the last two Roosevelt books, on Roosevelt's foreign policy, and let us say, read some of the recent attacks on Johnson's and Nixon's foreign policy, all you have to do is take Beard's text and simply change the names and you have pretty much the same things.

Commager: You do indeed, yes, for the revisionist school of the cause of the cold war.

Baughman: I see by our time that we have just a few moments but I see a hand in the audience. Would you like to ask a question?

Question: I am interested in this—do you find that Beard is a continuing influence? Do people go to Beard not, in 1974, to study history, or do scholars writing historical works go to him as a source? Do you just go to Beard to study Beard and not to study history?

Genovese: I think, as Mr. Commager suggested, the whole revisionist school in American diplomatic history derives very directly from Beard, his categories, his methods, the whole series of hypotheses he laid down. How well he might like their work is a question nobody can answer, but they have very self-consciously worked in his spirit and according to what they regard as the main lines of his interpretation. Now, beyond that, I think the question really asks something that is impossible because I don't see how it is possible for any American historian not to read Beard's work and to absorb all kinds of things from it—so much so that after a long period of development of different points of view and so on, I think we simply absorbed a great deal from Beard's work in forms no longer possible to isolate as specifically Beardian contributions. I would think that, in the long run, is the mark of a really great influential historian, after all his pet theories have been discarded and new facts have been brought up. The question is how much of his life's work has passed in these indirect channels into the mainstream of historical interpretation. For example, one can discard many of Gibbon's main theses on the decline of the Roman empire but I can't imagine, even today, computers or no computers, archaeology or no archaeology, that the most sophisticated historians of that period are not in all sorts of subtle ways influenced by his contribution to the writing of that history.

Commager: One additional thing, aside from what Mr. Genovese said, as it was said of Emerson, Beard was the cow from whom they all drew their milk. Certainly Beard was the cow from whom my generation drew its milk. Quite aside from that, he is also, to change the metaphor drastically, the King Charles' head of American historians. You can't get away from him; he's always there and if he's not there as an influence he's there as a counter-influence. First you have to dispose of him before you can get on with the job. That's not true of any other historians of our times, not even of Turner and Parrington, to anything like the same degree.

Baughman: Would you suspect, looking at this audience, that many of these people absorbed Beard and didn't realize it and today their own understanding of American history, as educated laymen but not necessarily historians, would be that of Beard?

Commager: Of course, he filters down into textbooks and to students of students of students, and he's everywhere and we're all Beardians in a way. We can't help ourselves. Whether we want to be or not, we're all Deweyites, we're all

Rousseauites. Everyone in this room owes an enormous
debt to Rousseau: no Rousseau, no John Dewey; no John
Dewey, no progressive education; and we are all victims of
progressive education—or beneficiaries, whatever it may
be. These things filter down, we don't even know where
they came from but they did come from the past mostly.
And Beard was a great figure whose teachings and ideas
and attitudes filtered down through my generation of
historians and then through Mr. Genovese's generation of
historians and his students.

Baughman: I am afraid we are going to
have, because of commit-
ments to airlines and so forth,
to close our panel. However,
there may be some of you who would like to address
questions personally to the members of the panel. I do
want to thank again the members of our profession who
have come here, the three gentlemen, Mr. Commager,
Professor Genovese and Professor Braeman, who have
brought to us this very stimulating two days of discussion
of Charles Beard. I believe some of you were not present
yesterday at the time that the family of Charles Beard was
introduced, and I know that many of you might care to
meet them and if they would not object again, I would like
to have the daughter of Charles and Mary Beard, Mrs.
Alfred Vagts, and the son, Dr. William Beard, and Charles
and Mary Beard's grandson, Professor Detlev Vagts, stand
for a moment and be recognized.

We are grateful for the many scholars who have come to
our campus to celebrate this centennial, to our alumni and
others who are here. I would like to say in behalf of my six
colleagues in the history department here at DePauw and
for myself that we are very proud to be a part of the
department that had as one of its great alumni Charles
Beard. We hope that we can continue in this tradition here
at DePauw and it is our ideal that maybe one of the young

people out there may be another Charles Beard. In conclusion, I would like to read a quotation from a newspaper. Charles Beard was editor of the *DePauw Palladium* , this was the school newspaper when he was here on campus and his last editorial in May of 1898, I think, gives us some indication of the young Beard as he moves on. If you can think with me here is Beard who has spent several years at DePauw, he is now leaving DePauw, he is leaving Greencastle, he's leaving Indiana and going on to England to his graduate studies and teaching at Columbia and to his very exciting and rewarding contributions to American life. And here is what he wrote in his last editorial on our campus:

> There is but one way to know the truth, and that is not a golden one. It is fraught with toil and sacrifice and perhaps ridicule. The seeker of the truth must be fearless, he must not be afraid to enter the innermost holies of holies, and to tear down the veils of super-stition that hang about any human and so-called divine institution. It is the truth that makes men free. If the truth tears down every church and government under the sun, let the truth be known and this truth only will be known when men cease to swallow the capsules of ancient doctors of divinities and politics; and when men begin to seek the truth in the records of history, politics and religion and science.

Charles A. Beard Centennial Committee

William E. Kerstetter, Chairman
Marvin C. Swanson, Co-ordinator

Stanley Caine
Elizabeth Christman
James L. Cooper
Robert H. Farber
David E. Horn
Clifton J. Phillips
Frederick A. Sanders
Gerald E. Warren
John B. Wilson